HARLEY-DAVIDSON

HARLEY-DAVIDSON

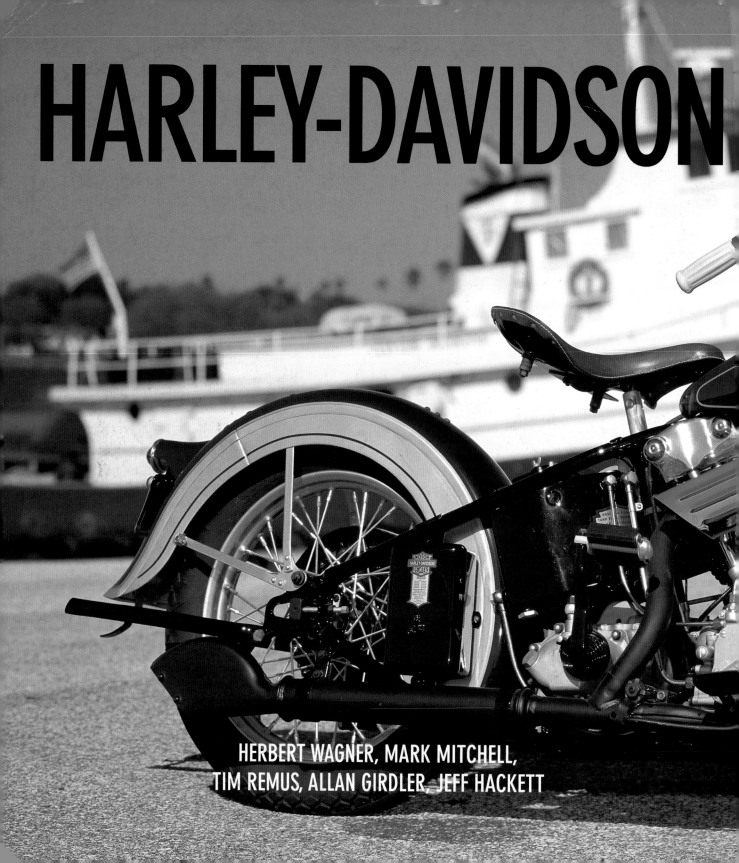

HERBERT WAGNER, MARK MITCHELL,
TIM REMUS, ALLAN GIRDLER, JEFF HACKETT

This edition published in 2003 by Lowe & B. Hould
Publishers, an imprint of Borders, Inc., 515 East Liberty,
Ann Arbor, MI 48104.
Lowe & B. Hould Publishers is a trademark of Borders
Properties, Inc.

First published by MBI Publishing Company, Galtier
Plaza, Suite 200, 380 Jackson Street, St. Paul, MN
55101-3885 USA

Classic Harley-Davidson: 1903–1941 © Herbert Wagner
 and Mark Mitchell, 1999
Harley-Davidson Customs © Tim Remus, 1995]
Harley-Davidson © Allan Girdler and Jeff Hackett, 2000

ISBN 0-681-01607-8

On the front cover: (Main) The Evolution V2 engine,
seen here in a custom-painted 1985 FXR, was traditional
in broad specs and in outline, but it was virtually
trouble-free.

(Right, top) The 1910 Model 6 was the last year of the
"Beehive"-style motor, enlarged in 1909 to 30.17 cubic
inches. The exhaust port had migrated toward the front
of the cylinder and a Shebler carburetor replaced H-D's
own make. Owner Walt Richie.

(Right, bottom) Denis Plante's V-twin retains its 80-ci
displacement, though it breathes through ported heads
with the help of an S&S cam and carburetor and a pair
of Bartels Performance pipes.

On the title page: In 1936, H-D created a masterpiece
with the 61 OHV, here illustrated by Mark Wall's
superbly restored 36EL1002.

On the back cover: New for the model year 2000 was
the Deuce—a play on numbers and words both—a
Softail with the counter-balanced beta version of the
Twin Cam 88 engine and a new, conservative sense of
style.

Printed in China

Contents

HARLEY-DAVIDSON

CLASSIC
HARLEY-DAVIDSON
1903-1941

HERBERT WAGNER

PHOTOGRAPHY BY
MARK MITCHELL

FOREWORD

Herbert Wagner is one of the few who can rightfully be called a historian. Scholars can obtain the facts—which Mr. Wagner does with precision—but only historians can reveal the narratives that facts will often conceal from the less inspired.

Classic Harley-Davidson, 1903–1941 is a remarkable book for its Logos and Mythos. During his investigations for this text, Herbert Wagner worked closely with the Harley-Davidson Archives to study primary and secondary materials that would not have been available elsewhere, and to converse with Archives personnel with whom many spirited discussions took place regarding the materials. Some of Wagner's findings were so serendipitous that upon discovery he said to me, "Marty, the ghost just walked through the room!"

Information on historical overhead-valve technology was, I believe, the moment when Herbert's ghost was released, but it could have been set free to haunt during any number of his discoveries. The Archives' antique motorcycle, photograph, literature, and ephemera collections contain the very essence of the phenomenon we all know as Harley-Davidson.

I am pleased that it could be utilized for this book, and now it is time for you, the reader, to let the ghost walk through your room as you read Herbert Wagner's brilliant historical incantation.

Dr. Martin Jack Rosenblum
Historian
Harley-Davidson Motor Company

ACKNOWLEDGMENTS

The author's historical research on the Harley-Davidson Motor Co. has been conducted continuously since 1988. Material for this book came from a variety of published and unpublished sources. The latter includes letters, taped interviews, original factory data, notes, photographs, and other information from the author's files.

The author wishes to thank the following persons for assistance with the present book: Mrs. Bill Borer, Bob Chantland, Alfred Embretsen, Greg Field, Aaron Fitch (of the Motorcycle Heritage Museum), Herb Glass, Chris Haynes, Bob Jameson, Mark Jonas, Tom Jorsch, Akemi Somon Kobayashi, Walter Kobs, Joe Koller, Rachel Amara Landman, Arnold Meyer Jr., Fritz Meyer, Mark

Mitchell and Rebecca Dobyns. Rick Morsher. Elizabeth Durr Moyle. Adolph Roemer. Phil Runser (of Advanced Cycle Machining). the late George Sceets. Connie Schlemmer. Dr. Mark Sneed. Joseph Somogyi family. Daniel Statnekov. Grace Kobs Valsano. Howard Vandegrift. the late Tom Vandegrift. Mrs. Walter Waech. Mark Wall. Tom Wagner. the late John Warner. and Dick Werner.

Special thanks to the John E. Harley family for preserving and sharing the 1901 engine drawing. R. L. Jones for information on hillclimbers and early racers. Mike Lange for his intimate knowledge of early Harley engines. Bruce Linsday for his expertise on the first Harleys and his boundless enthusiasm for Knuckleheads. Floyd Smith for help on the classic hillclimbing scene. and to Chuck Wesholski for introducing me to the super-important Two-Cam/OHV and straightening me out about the Knuth's Special.

And last. but certainly not least. thanks to Tom Bolfert. Bill Jackson. Dr. Martin Jack Rosenblum. and Ray Schlee for their great assistance at the Harley-Davidson Archives on Juneau Avenue in Milwaukee.

—*Herbert Wagner*

INTRODUCTION

Between 1903 and 1941 the modern Harley-Davidson motorcycle came into existence. From a spindly. single-cylinder razorstrap job. the Harley grew into the 74 OHV Big Twin— the Knucklehead—a fast. reliable roadburner still worthy of the pavement today.

This development began shortly after the close of the American frontier. Having conquered the lower 48 states. that restless American spirit set out to invent the best means of exploring them. For four young men in Milwaukee. Wisconsin. this meant the motorcycle. By 1941 their motorized bicycle had become an iron horse.

Yet mysteries remain about Harley-Davidson's early history. What originally inspired Bill Harley and Arthur Davidson to build a motorcycle? What did their 1901 motor-bicycle engine look like? Where did the big motor and loop frame of 1903 come from? When was the first twin built? Why did Harley-Davidson grow so quickly in the early years? What part did World War I play? When did the image of the anti-social biker first appear? Why was the 21-cubic-inch Single significant? What unknown experimental model inspired the Knucklehead? When were the first Knuckleheads shipped from the factory? Was there a single-cylinder Knucklehead?

This book tries to answer these and other questions in the colorful setting of Mark Mitchell's photographs. The history of Harley-Davidson might be termed a mechanical romance. In these pages. I've attempted to explore a part of that romance for Harley-Davidson enthusiasts everywhere.

CHAPTER 1
PENNINGTON'S MOTORCYCLE,
TWO FRENCHMEN, AND
THE 1901 BICYCLE MOTOR

In another life, Bill Harley might have been an artist and Arthur Davidson a cattle rancher. But things turned out differently. For in the summer of 1895, Edward Joel "Airship" Pennington touched down in Milwaukee with his fabulous new invention: the "Motor Cycle."

This was the day of the bicycle craze, and millions of American men and women were on wheels. But the bicycle was limited to the power in one's legs. Hills were a bitch. Some dreamers were asking for the seemingly impossible: a motorized bicycle.

> ## "The greatest possibilities are with the bicycle, driven by electric power or compressed air, by which means . . . fifty miles an hour will soon be reached."
> —Alfred Wallace, 1896
> *The Wonderful Century*

Over the years, there had been a few steam-powered velocipedes. In 1885 Germany, Daimler had built a gasoline-powered hobby-horse, but with four wheels this device was not a true motorcycle. H-D's historian, Marty Rosenblum, has aptly dubbed it "the first Volkswagen."

Nor did these early freaks capture the imagination of the dreamers, those who grasped the essence of a true motorcycle: light, strong, nimble, powerful, fast, and handsome. As if answering their prayers, Pennington arrived, messiah-like, with his prophetic Motor Cycle.

This Indiana-born inventor-promoter had invented a compact type of gasoline engine he then fitted to the rear frame section of a bicycle. The connecting rods operated, locomotive-style, directly upon the rear wheel hub. Pennington claimed that his 12-pound engine produced 2 horsepower.

The French de Dion-Bouton engine set the pattern for the first successful motorcycles. This 1 3/4-horsepower 1899 example with close-set rear wheels is owned by Reed Martin and was ordered by the Vanderbilts for use as a bicycle pacer.

13

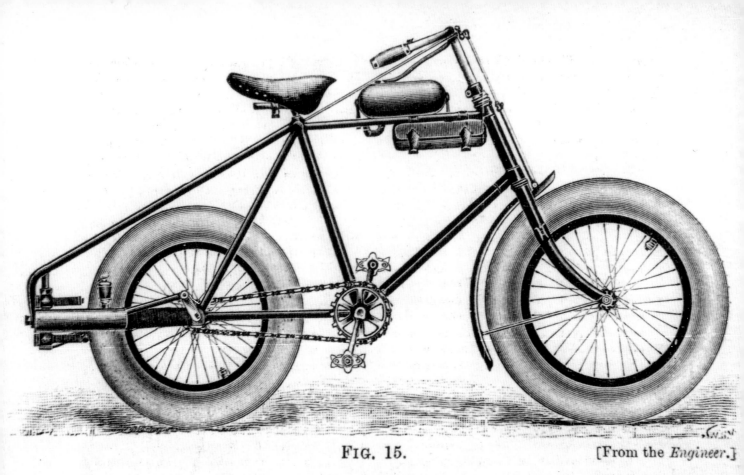

FIG. 15.

[From the *Engineer.*]

Pennington's "Motor Cycle" was seen in several American cities before it came to Milwaukee in 1895. Bill Harley and Arthur Davidson—then both 14 years old—lived just a few blocks from where the Motor Cycle was publicly demonstrated. *AUTHOR COLLECTION*

Loud, crude, and imperfect, the Motor Cycle drew crowds wherever it went. By 1890s standards, it moved with "lightning-like rapidity," according to one Milwaukee newspaper. It held infinite possibilities at a time when the bicycle itself bordered upon the magical.

In Milwaukee, Pennington made two dashes up and down Wisconsin Avenue, leaving the street awash in a haze of poorly combusted hydrocarbons, raw gasoline, the bark of exhaust, and Pennington's own booming bombast. Police could scarcely hold back the crowd. Later, Pennington claimed that he did 58 miles per hour in Milwaukee—his best speed to date.

At this point an important historical question arises: Who was in the crowd that day? For just a few blocks from this fantastic 1890s scene there lived two families named Harley and Davidson.

William Sylvester Harley and Arthur Davidson were boyhood chums. In 1895 they were 14 years old. At this impressionable age both were keenly interested in mechanical things and optimistic for the birth of a new century.

It's hardly conceivable that two young Milwaukee lads, living near the scene of Pennington's ride, failed to witness this historic event. Subsequent Harley-Davidson histories tell of a dream these two boys had of building a motorized bicycle long before they actually did so. Might this dream have sprouted from their encounter with that knuckle-head genius E. J. Pennington?

But the Motor Cycle of 1895 was a flash on the horizon, then gone. After that one-day visit, Milwaukee settled back into its late-19th-century beery slumber.

But events had been set in motion. The next year the Harley family moved to the north side where young William found employment at the Meiselbach bicycle factory. The Davidsons moved to the city's western outskirts, and Art went to Cambridge, Wisconsin, where he lived on his grandmother's farm. There he met another gasoline-sniffing pioneer, Ole Oleson Evinrude.

Across the ocean, other developments were taking place that would transform the motorcycle from a charlatan's contraption into a practical device. This achievement was due to two Frenchmen: the brilliant Comte Albert de Dion and his wizard-like mechanic, Georges Bouton.

Confident that the future of *l'idée automobile* rested in gasoline, de Dion and former-toy-maker Bouton began experimenting with the Daimler-Maybach version of Otto's four-stroke engine. Using hot-tube ignition, Daimler's vertical, all-enclosed 212 cc engine produced 1/2 horsepower at 600 rpm, but weighed 189 pounds.

De Dion and Bouton did better. By miniaturizing Daimler's motor, they created an air-cooled engine that weighed just 40 pounds. They also developed a new form of battery/spark ignition utilizing a cam-activated circuit breaker run off the engine. Now the spark could keep pace with the piston as rpm increased. This allowed the de Dion-Bouton engine to spin at unheard-of rates. When tested in 1895, this 137 cc engine took off like a rocket to 3,000 rpm and ran *reliably* at 1,500, producing about 1/2 horsepower.

A revolution in gasoline engineering had taken place. With the de Dion-Bouton engine the modern motorcycle was possible. Every bike engine today is derived from this motor. Ironically, Pennington later claimed that *his* engine had inspired de Dion-Bouton's work, but this was probably wishful thinking.

After 1896, de Dion tricycles and quadracycles filled Paris boulevards. French motor-bicycles appeared in 1897. This new technology reached the United States in 1898, with clones of the de Dion trike. But trikes couldn't easily negotiate rutted American roads. Two-wheelers could. The first *successful* American motorcycles—the Thomas, Marsh, and Orient—appeared in late 1900. Predictably, these bikes showed a strong French influence, as would the first Indian.

By this time Bill Harley was an apprentice draftsman at the Barth Manufacturing Co. Writing to his pal Art Davidson out on the farm, he told of the big demand for skilled workers in Milwaukee's booming industries. Taking Harley's advice, Art came home and became an apprentice pattern maker.

One evening they went to the Bijou Theater and witnessed Anna Held, the Parisian-born comedienne, whiz across the stage on a nickel-plated French motor-bicycle.

The eyes of our young titans bugged out at the sight of this "shapely damsel in white tights" maneuvering around the stage. As they recalled 41 years later in the *Milwaukee Journal*, "It was just one of those many little things that push people further toward a goal they are groping for."

The motorcycle of 1900 had not yet reached Milwaukee streets, but with this new inspiration, Bill Harley and Arthur Davidson decided to build their own.

It was an ambitious project to start from scratch. Luckily, do-it-yourself engine kits were becoming available. From a magazine ad you could purchase the rough castings and on a lathe make motor shafts and other parts. You could then clamp the finished engine onto a bicycle and drive it with belt and pulley. Harley and Davidson apparently took this first step in their career of building motorcycles.

A 1914 newspaper article tells that a German-born "draughtsman," working in the same machine shop as our heroes, gave them valuable technical advice on gasoline engines. Another break came when Henry Melk, a pal in Bill Harley's neighborhood, let them use his lathe.

Facts were sketchy about this first Harley-Davidson motor until 1997, when an engineering drawing of it surfaced. This oldest known H-D relic

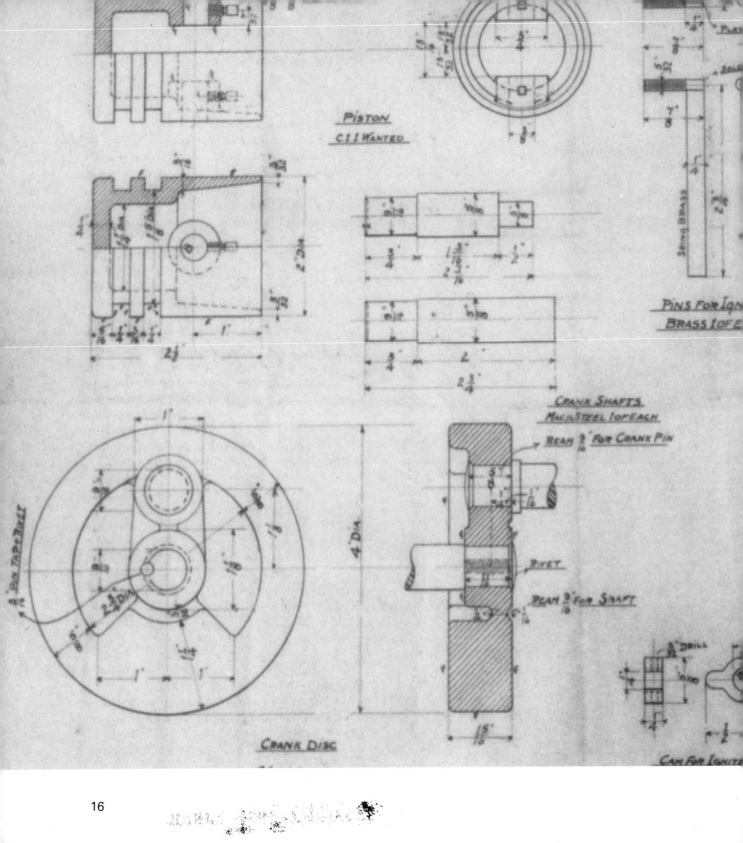

PISTON

C.I. 1 WANTED

PINS FOR IGN

BRASS 1 OF E

CRANK SHAFTS

MAC'L STEEL 1 OF EACH

REAM $\frac{9}{16}$ FOR CRANK PIN

RIVET

REAM $\frac{9}{16}$ FOR SHAFT

CRANK DISC

CAM FOR IGNITO

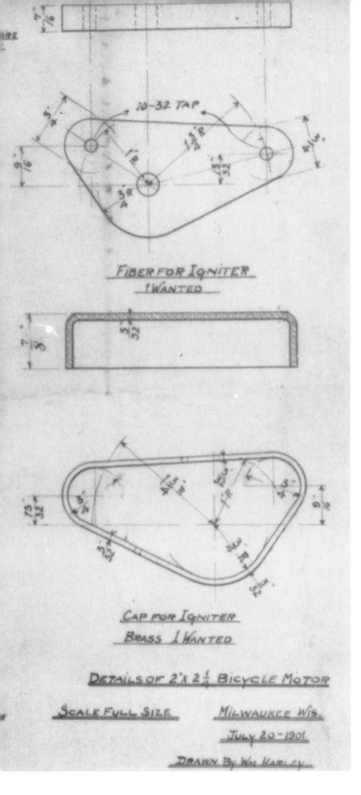

FIBER FOR IGNITER
1 WANTED

CAP FOR IGNITER
BRASS 1 WANTED

DETAILS OF 2" x 2¼ BICYCLE MOTOR

SCALE FULL SIZE   MILWAUKEE WIS.

JULY 20 - 1901

DRAWN BY WM. HARLEY.

is dated July 20, 1901, and is signed by William S. Harley. The drawing is labeled "Sheet 2," and shows several parts of the bicycle motor. For unknown reasons its 2x2 1/4-inch bore and stroke (7.068 cubic inches or 115.8 cc) with 4-inch flywheels differs from those described in the 1914 *Milwaukee Journal* article, which states, "the first motor had a bore of 2 1/8 inches and a stroke of 2 7/8 inches, the fly wheel being 5 inches in diameter."

The 1901 drawing does show, however, that production Harley-Davidson engines of 1903–1905 were *not* enlarged versions of this first design. A comparison between the dimensions on the cast parts versus the machined parts suggests that this 1901 engine was built around a purchased kit. Early-Harley expert Bruce Linsday observed, "Looks like [Harley] measured the castings he had in his hand, and was pretty vague on the machined parts that still had to be made."

This kit approach to engine building was a logical choice for two young guys with little money, no experience, and access only to Henry Melk's lathe. Ambition, however, they had in abundance, and late in 1901 they installed the motor in an ordinary bicycle chassis and tested their invention. To their dismay they found it too weakly powered for climbing Milwaukee's steeper hills.

We can only imagine their disappointment. By then—late 1901—motorcycles were reality on Milwaukee streets, where A. J. Monday was handling the Thomas brand. In nearby Racine, the Wisconsin Wheel Works was turning out the Mitchell motorcycle. On Milwaukee's south side, Joe Merkel was building Merkel motorcycles.

At that juncture Bill Harley and Art Davidson might have thrown in the towel. Why should they build a motorcycle of their own when they could just go out and buy one?

This engineering drawing signed by William S. Harley is dated July 20, 1901. It shows parts for a 7.07-cubic-inch (116 cc) bicycle motor. When put into a frame, this engine was found lacking in power for Milwaukee hills, but inspired bigger motors to come. *Photo courtesy John E. Harley family*

CHAPTER 2
THE 1903 PROTOTYPE

Bill Harley and Arthur Davidson weren't easily discouraged. Davidson. a brassy little guy. was no quitter. Building a motorcycle was more art than science anyway. and there was plenty of artist in Bill Harley.

The motor-bicycle project had given them valuable experience. Examining the motorcycles being built. they were determined to do better next time. Plus they had friends. Among them was a man who later became famous for outboard motors. Ole Evinrude.

Ole was three years older than Bill Harley and Arthur Davidson and considerably more worldly. He had worked in machine shops in Madison. Pittsburgh. and Chicago. Nights. he studied books on gasoline engineering. and soon he began experimenting.

By 1902. Ole was in business with Frank Clemick on Florida Street in Milwaukee. The Clemick-Evinrude Co. billed themselves as "pattern makers and engine builders." Their engine

> "Everyone . . . was fooling around with motors and gasoline that evaporated faster than it drove those motors. Nothing ran smoothly but the whole thing was exciting, like coming into a new world of green valleys and blue mountains."
>
> —Gustave Pabst, Jr.

was Ole's adaptation of the de Dion-Bouton type—in water-cooled form—for automotive use.

At that time Ole was developing an improved engine. In 1903. he formed a new partnership to market it with Ferdy Achtenhagen at 255 Lake Street. This was the Motor Car Power Equipment Co.

Here's where things got interesting. Not only was Ole a friend of Art Davidson from their Cambridge days. but Art was also a "partner" in Ole's pattern shop around this time. Just two blocks away. Bill Harley was working at Pawling & Harnischfeger.

Since 1914. Harley-Davidson has given credit to Evinrude for helping our heroes get a start. usually with their carburetor. But Ole's help appears to have gone deeper. Several unique features of Evinrude's improved motor are found in early Harley-Davidson engines. These include the hand starter. two-piece exhaust valve. side exhaust port. roller tappet. and oil routing system to the crankpin. The last two features are still used on Harley-Davidson engines today.

Coincidence? Not likely. considering the close connections between these guys. It's easy to surmise what happened. With the puny 1901 motor a failure. big-hearted Ole probably encouraged Bill Harley to draft plans for an air-cooled cycle engine from his larger water-cooled design. A case of one great man helping another get his start.

"Negative 599." This circa-1912 photo was labeled "1903 Harley-Davidson" and shows a bike with pre-1905 features. The spring fork was added later. The bike was probably sold in 1904 to Henry Meyer and by 1912 had accumulated 100,000 miles. Its current whereabouts are unknown. *Photo courtesy Milwaukee County Historical Society*

19

The timing is right. Both men were working on new engines in 1902; both finished them in 1903. Yet, while showing strong Evinrude influence, the H-D was not a direct copy. The Evinrude motor was water-cooled and larger, the crankcases were heavier and reinforced, and lubrication was by oil cup. It should also be remembered that all these early engines were copies of the de Dion-Bouton, which in turn was based on Daimler's design.

The improved Harley-Davidson motor of 1902–1903 more than doubled the displacement of the previous bicycle motor. Bore and stroke were 3x3 1/2 inches, yielding 24.74 cubic inches (405 cc). The flywheels were 9 3/4 inches, *not* 11 1/2 inches as incorrectly reported in 1914 and repeated ever since. Output was about 3 horsepower.

With an engine worthy of the name "Harley-Davidson," our young mechanics were eager to push ahead—only to discover a new hurdle.

The 1901 motor had been small enough to install on an ordinary bicycle frame, standard practice at that time. But at 49 pounds, the 1902–1903 motor was too large for similar treatment. Luckily, rapid advances in the local motorcycle industry provided the answer. Thereby hangs an untold tale, and a big part of Harley-Davidson's early success.

The big name in the early motorcycle industry was the Indian Motocycle Co. of Springfield, Massachusetts. With its low-slung engine inline with the seat post in a bicycle-style diamond frame, the Indian was maneuverable, light, and speedy. The original 1901 design was so successful that Indian stuck to it until 1909, long after it was obsolete.

The Merkel motorcycle was built in Milwaukee between 1901 and 1908. The first Harley may have been inspired by the re-designed 1903 model, as the frames are nearly identical and overall styling very similar. No examples of this model Merkel is known to survive. *Author collection*

In the Milwaukee area, however, the two earliest builders took a less successful initial approach. Both the (Milwaukee) Merkel and (Racine) Mitchell models of 1901–1902 utilized bicycle-style frames with high-mounted engines. While racy looking, these proved a devil for sideslip.

Consequently, both these companies came out with entirely new designs for 1903. These new Merkel and Mitchell machines were highly advanced, second-generation mounts. Abandoning the diamond-shaped bicycle chassis, both firms introduced frames in which the engine was the integral heart of the vehicle instead of showing a tacked-on bicycle approach. This design philosophy is universally followed today.

The 1903 Merkel used the classic "loop frame" style where the front down tube wrapped around the engine crankcase and then looped up as the seat post. The 1903 Mitchell utilized a slightly different "cradle frame" in which the front down tube flowed back as the rear frame-stay instead of that section being added separately. Both makes mounted their engines low and with a forward cant to allow better cylinder cooling.

The innovative 1903 Merkel and Mitchell designs took into account the physics of mating the gasoline engine to the two-wheeler. Forward thinkers realized that motorcycles were not motorized bicycles, but unique vehicles with their own demands and solutions.

Here, too, timing is significant. In late 1902, when these advanced designs were being introduced by Milwaukee-area factories, Bill Harley and

Arthur Davidson were searching for a better chassis for their improved motor. They apparently found it in the Merkel loop frame, as the early Harley-Davidson frame is a dead ringer.

This is all vital stuff. It allowed the prototype Harley-Davidson of 1903 to appear as a second-generation mount—a true motorcycle utilizing the best of current theory and practice. With a superior engine and frame, Harley-Davidson was propelled rapidly forward while others were struggling with underpowered, obsolete, or freakish designs.

Patterns for the improved model were made by Arthur Davidson, based on Bill Harley's drawings. Machine work was done on Henry Melk's lathe. It's also likely that Art's older brother, William A. Davidson, began lending a hand as well. Real old-timers still chuckle when they recall Bill Davidson—in 1903 the toolroom foreman at the West Milwaukee car shops of the Chicago, Milwaukee & St. Paul Railway—telling how parts for the first Harley were fabricated at the railroad. He jokingly referred to it as "government work."

This makes perfect sense. Material had to be obtained. Parts such as the flywheels called for big equipment. Others had to be cast. The flywheel cutouts in early H-D motors resemble a locomotive's drive wheel. Coincidence? Maybe, but consider how many skilled men later followed Bill Davidson from the railroad, and it's no mystery that much of the first Harley came out of the railshops. Today, these buildings stand as ruins below the 35th Street viaduct in Milwaukee.

The individual parts were assembled into a complete motorcycle in the backyard "woodshed" of the Davidson family home at 315 37th Street (now 38th Street). The shed was originally built by the Davidson boys' father, William C. Davidson, for his own use, but was soon taken over by his sons and Bill Harley.

Early histories tell that in April 1903, Walter Davidson came back to Milwaukee for brother Bill's marriage to Mary Bauer. Walter was enticed to join their budding motorcycle-building enterprise by the promise of a ride. One 1916 source largely credits Walter with building the 1903 prototype.

Their new machine drew considerable attention. From nearby Vliet Street, the Becker boys started

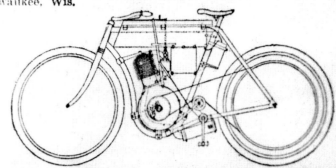

Harley-Davidson Motor Cycle
Made by Harley-Davidson Motor Co., 315 37th St., Milwaukee, **Wis.**

HARLEY-DAVIDSON MOTOR CYCLE. PRICE $175.

21½-inch frame; 2-inch tires, but option is given on 2¼-inch; 51½-inch wheel base; single cylinder, 3⅛x3½, 3¼ H. P. motor; centrifugal sight feed lubrication;

This line drawing, published in April 1905, may portray the first Harley-Davidson or the 1904 factory racer. It is the earliest known visual representation of a Harley-Davidson motorcycle and another of Bill Harley's artistic renderings. AUTHOR COLLECTION

hanging around. Interested guys from the railshops, such as Max Kobs, stopped by, as did schoolyard chums like Henry Meyer. Everybody lent a hand when needed and had plenty of advice to offer.

With this encouragement, the first Harley-Davidson was successfully tested in late 1903. Ten years later Bill Harley recalled the launching: "You should have seen the spark plug—as big as a door knob. And they cost us $3 each. . . . I have had a good many laughs since whenever I think of those door knob spark plugs."

It's difficult for us today to imagine the thrill this new world of motorcycles possessed. With just a little gasoline you were zooming along effortlessly toward the setting sun. The burden of pedaling had been conquered.

With the completion of their motorcycle, Bill Harley and the Davidson brothers had accomplished their task. They may have planned to fabricate another example or two so they all could ride, but surely this would be the end of their motorcycle building. Now their spare time could be spent on great outdoor adventures.

21

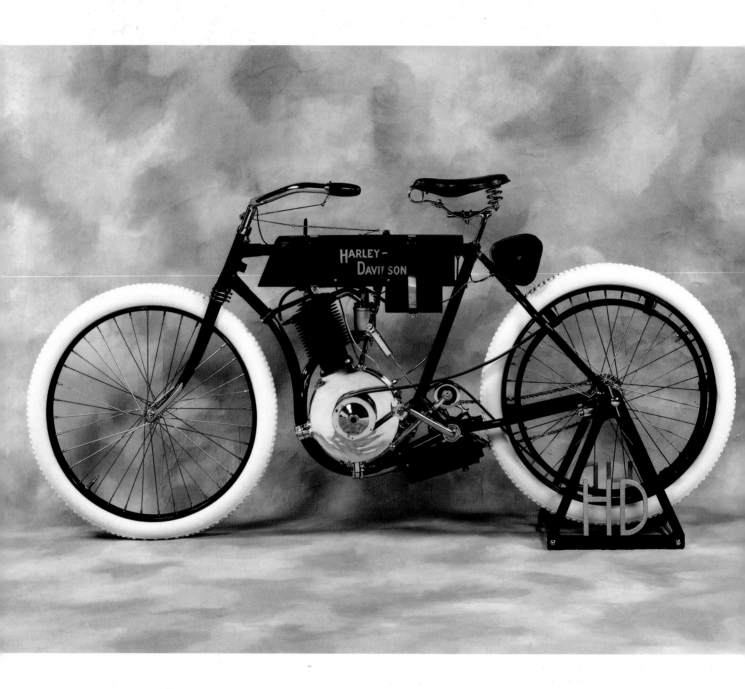

CHAPTER 3
EARLY SINGLES

Thus far, creating the Harley-Davidson motorcycle had been a hobby. Then Henry Meyer got tired of walking to his job at the woolen mill and offered to buy that first 1903 machine.

This opened our heroes' eyes. The motorcycle, relatively simple to build and lower cost, was seen as a poor man's automobile. Others wanted motorcycles for speed thrills. Whatever the reason, demand outstripped supply, and overnight a hobby became an enterprise.

This resulted in the Harley-Davidson Motor Co. being formed as a partnership. Not that it meant much. All involved kept their day jobs except for Bill Harley who, realizing that he would need an engineering background to succeed in this new gasoline-powered world order, packed his spare shirt and enrolled at the University of Wisconsin in late 1903.

In 1904, one or two more Harley-Davidsons were assembled. Some claim eight, but that seems overly optimistic. They really got going in 1905. In January, and for several months thereafter, a 1-inch

"We are now offering . . . a motor that is very powerful . . . that will stand the hardest of usage with a minimum of repair."

—1905 H-D sales brochure

advertisement for "Harley-Davidson Motor Cycle Motors" was run in the *Cycle and Automobile Trade Journal*. A sales brochure was also prepared.

It's unknown how many bare motors were sold in 1905. One order from Nebraska called for fifty. Some motors were used to power boats on Pewaukee Lake.

A 1905 Harley-Davidson engine sold for $60 (carburetor $10 extra). It weighed 49 pounds—24 pounds in the motor's hefty flywheels. Good workmanship and high-quality materials were evident. Motors could be ordered with a drive pulley of 4 1/2-, 5 1/4-, or 6-inch diameter—all for use with a 1 1/4-inch flat belt. Unusual for a motorcycle engine was its provision for a hand-crank starter.

The cylinder, head, and valve chamber were integrally cast of "fine gray" iron with 1-inch cooling fins. The crankcase was made of nickel aluminum and fitted with phosphor-bronze plain bearings.

The connecting rod was constructed with a split bearing at the crank pin for taking up wear. The piston had three rings cut with a lap joint and re-turned to fit the cylinder bore.

Lubrication was by "centrifugal feed" where oil was fed by gravity from the tank to the crankpin bearing via drilled flywheel and motor shaft. From there, oil was thrown by centrifugal

For decades this racy little number was hidden behind fenders and other incorrect parts. New research led to the stunning transformation shown here. Opinions on year of manufacture vary from 1903 to 1905. *HARLEY-DAVIDSON ARCHIVES*

force to the various working parts of the motor. The system was described as "simple and efficient" with little danger of flooding the cylinder with oil.

The spark plug was placed in the side of the combustion chamber where it was less prone to fouling and overheating. The ignition circuit breaker ("interrupter") consisted of two platinum points operated by a hardened cam.

Valve openings were reported in 1905 as being 1 3/16 inches in diameter. The inlet valve was steel, while the exhaust valve had a steel stem and a cast-iron head to resist scaling. Both valves in the 1905 motor were reported as having flat seats.

From its Daimler and de Dion-Bouton ancestry, the H-D engine inherited the inlet-valve-over-exhaust-valve, head-cylinder design. Obsolete today, the IOE or F-head valve layout was used universally in the pioneer days.

In this engine type, the valves were located in an adjacent chamber or pocket at the top of the

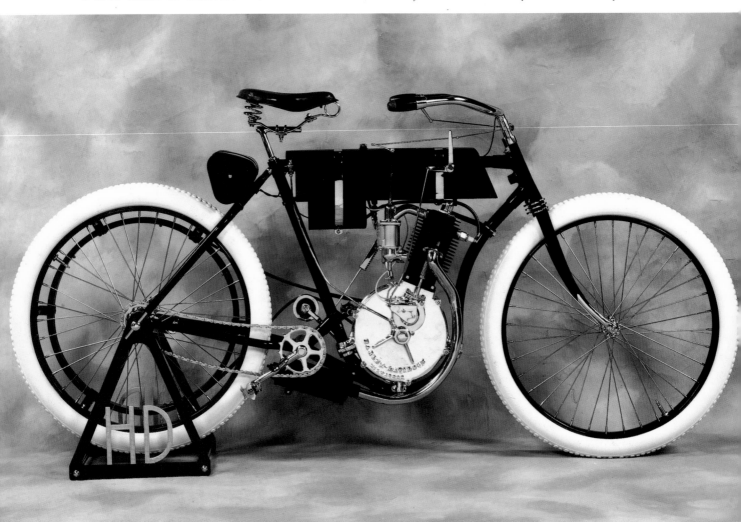

As now restored, this early Harley resembles the engineering line drawing done by Bill Harley before April 1905. Small number "1"s on several parts led H-D to name the bike "Serial Number One." See related sidebar on page 25.

HARLEY-DAVIDSON ARCHIVES

The side exhaust and internal features of the 1905 single suggest help from Ole Evinrude. Black was standard fare in 1905 with Renault gray an option in 1906. *Bike courtesy H-D Archives.*

cylinder. The exhaust valve was aligned parallel with the bore and faced upward into the combustion chamber, while the inlet valve was positioned directly over the exhaust valve with its head facing downward into the combustion chamber. This was a practical design with several advantages— one being that fresh incoming fuel cooled the exhaust valve head, thereby reducing its temperature and failure rate.

A peculiar feature of these early F-head engines was their "automatic"-type inlet valve.

Held closed by a weak spring, the inlet valve was opened during the intake stroke of the piston when vacuum in the chamber overpowered the tension of the weak spring, opening the valve and allowing the fresh fuel charge to be sucked in. The exhaust valve was mechanically operated by a cam and closed by spring pressure, as in modern practice.

Changes were already evident between the 1903–1904 Harley-Davidson engine and the model of 1905. The previous autumn, Arthur Davidson made new patterns, and the engine was slightly

Big crankcases contain 9 3/4-inch flywheels, not 11-inch as widely reported. Heavy flywheels and relatively large displacement gave the first Harleys "lugging" advantage over the competition on poor roads.

In June 1905, Perry E. Mack (possibly H-D's first employee) set a speed record on a local track riding a 1905 model. Afterwards (a local paper stated), Arthur Davidson walked around "swelled up like a toy balloon." This event spurred them to drop the bare motor trade for a serious attempt at building complete motorcycles.

Another impetus came when Carl Herman Lang of Chicago was in Milwaukee on business and saw their advanced motorcycle. Already a motorcycle buff, Lang offered to be their Chicago agent. Production in 1905 was probably five bikes and Lang took three, thereby becoming the world's first Harley-Davidson dealer.

These events explain why Harley's early numbering system used 1905 as base-year one. This lasted until 1916, when the current year method was adopted. Thus, a 1915 bike was designated "Model 11," 1914 bikes "Model 10," and so on back to 1905 and "Model 1." Harley-Davidson considered 1903–1904 bikes prototypes, not production machines.

Bare motor ads disappeared in mid-1905. Later that year, H-D issued its first motorcycle sales brochure with illustrations of a 1905 model. The brochure was undated and intended to serve for an indefinite period.

Bikes were offered in black in 1905, with Renault gray an option in 1906. With its motor "hung low" in the frame, the Harley-Davidson was advertised as being "especially strong to stand the rough American roads." The three-coil saddle promised to make "an ideal, easy riding machine for touring." Cost of the 1905 model was $200.

Compared to local and national competitors, the Harley-Davidson stood up well:

redesigned. Engine mounting lugs were spaced farther apart for greater strength and the bore was increased from 3 to 3 1/8 inches for more power. This provided the 1905 motor with 26.84 cubic inches (440 cc), developing 3 1/4 horsepower.

In 1905, the Motor Company laid down its design philosophy by stating in its sales brochure: "Experience has shown that it is preferable to use a comparatively large motor running at a moderate speed in preference to a smaller motor running at high speed."

These first singles laid the foundation for subsequent Harley-Davidson engines. The bottom end in these early motors bears a haunting resemblance to Harley-Davidson engines today.

Belonging to the Harley Archives, and on display at the Milwaukee Public Museum, this 1907 model shows the gradual updating that marked subsequent H-D engineering history. The spring fork appears to be from a 1908 model.

Selected 1905 Models
(Cycle and Automobile Trade Journal)

Mitchell *(Racine, Wis.)*
Motor: 38.48 cubic inches (630 cc)
Output: 4 horsepower
Frame: cradle
Wheelbase: 55 inches
Weight: 160 pounds
Drive: chain washer belt
Top speed: 60 miles per hour

Harley-Davidson *(Milwaukee, Wis.)*
Motor: 26.84 cubic inches (440 cc)
Output: 3 1/4 horsepower
Frame: loop
Wheelbase: 51 inches
Weight: 138 pounds
Drive: flat belt
Top speed: 50 miles per hour

Indian *(Springfield, Mass.)*
Motor: 15.85 cubic inches (260 cc)
Output: 1 3/4 horsepower
Frame: diamond
Wheelbase: (not available)
Weight: 110 pounds
Drive: chain
Top speed: 40 miles per hour

Merkel *(Milwaukee, Wis.)*
Motor: 15.56 cubic inches (255 cc)
Output: 2 1/4 horsepower
Frame: loop
Wheelbase: 50 inches
Weight: 108 pounds
Drive: flat belt
Top speed: 35 miles per hour

This close-up view of a 1907 engine reveals subtle differences from the 1905 version. Six-bolt crankcases were found on 1906 and earlier motors, while 1907 and later had eight-bolt crankcases. Cast-in name and motor-mount position were also changed.

WORLD'S OLDEST HARLEY

The oldest motorcycle in the Harley-Davidson Archives' bike collection is well known to enthusiasts both from photographs and its display in the lobby at the Juneau Avenue headquarters.

Few questioned the lobby bike's authenticity until it was examined by Harley's professional restorer Ray Schlee in preparation for H-D's 95th Anniversary. Schlee was aided in his research on the bike by H-D's historian Marty Rosenblum and outside experts Bruce Linsday and Mike Lange. The author also contributed his two cents worth.

Based on their findings, Schlee's restoration resulted in the stunning machine pictured on pages 18 and 19. Previously, the bike had an endearing but clunky look. It was discovered, however, upon disassembly, that the bike originally had no fenders and that other key parts were incorrect, including both seat and handlebars. In addition, the engine had a higher compression than other existing pre-1906 engines, suggesting—of all things—a racing motor!

These findings were difficult to reconcile with the lobby bike's traditional configuration, save for two significant findings: First, an engineering line drawing done by William S. Harley before April 1905 shows a Harley-Davidson motorcycle *without* fenders, with low handlebars, and a low racing seat.

Second, the recently documented fact that Harley-Davidson had raced a bike in the autumn of 1904. Tying these two things together is the opinion of experts like Bruce Linsday who believes that Bill Harley's line drawing portrayed an early racer.

H-D's historian Marty Rosenblum (standing) and old-bike expert Ray Schlee played key roles in transforming the world's oldest Harley to its current, more authentic form. They are shown here with the Archives' 1905 model.

While the pros don't usually base full restorations on a solitary drawing, and Motor Company policy is to preserve, not restore, Archives bikes, this was a special case. Harley-Davidson wanted total authenticity in a bike known to be incorrect, probably dating back to circumstances in 1915 when the collection nucleus was assembled.

The line drawing—done by Bill Harley himself—was obviously authentic. Plus it was impossible to ignore the many incongruities on the lobby bike that seemed to match the line drawing bike. What tipped the scales, perhaps, was the fact that Harley raced in late 1904, and the lobby bike's motor seemed to be a racing engine. Was it possible that the stodgy old lobby bike was actually *Harley's first racer?*

As a result of these factors (and with considerable trepidation because you don't mess lightly with Harley-Davidson tradition), Schlee restored the lobby bike with a new and different look—one more in line with Bill Harley's early drawing. Depending on the bike's date of manufacture (opinions vary between 1903 and 1905), it may be the very machine ridden by Edward Hildebrand in the 1904 race. As noted previously, the higher compression motor does suggest a competition machine.

Several small number "1"s appearing on certain parts have led to serious discussion about whether this bike was the first in some series. While questions are likely to remain about this earliest known Harley, it now sports its (probable) original racy look. Whoever dreamed the first Harleys were such cool little hot rods?

The 1910 Model 6 was the last year of the "Beehive"-style motor, enlarged in 1909 to 30.17 cubic inches (495 cc). The exhaust port had migrated toward the front of the cylinder and a Schebler carburetor replaced H-D's own make. Owner Walt Richie.

New for 1910 was an improved belt tensioner with working parts behind the pulley. A single movement of the lever engaged the engine to the drive belt but was still not a practical clutch. Pedal-assist was used for the first few feet to get things rolling.

Although history books state otherwise, the Harley-Davidson engine was *not* the largest single-cylinder motor used in early American motorcycles. That distinction belongs to the "monstrous mile-a-minute Mitchell," displacing 36 percent *more* swept piston volume than the Harley. The only thing bigger in 1905 was the 42.41-cubic-inch (695 cc) Curtiss V-twin.

The Harley's appeal is evident, however, when compared to the obsolete yet popular Indian design and the advanced but sedate Merkel. The Mitchell—a real he-man's machine—was dropped in 1906 when the company shifted emphasis to auto building. After a short, disastrous foray into the auto industry, Joe Merkel left Milwaukee in 1908. But before the local industry fell apart, an interesting event took place.

Back in the autumn of 1904, a Harley-Davidson motorcycle had gone up against the Mitchell, Merkel, and other makes in the first race ever run by a Harley-Davidson motorcycle. Ridden by Edward Hildebrand, the Harley beat several makes, including the Milwaukee Merkel. But in both races the Harley was bested, first by Frank X. Zirbes of Racine on a Mitchell, and in the other by Paul Stamser of Muskegon, Michigan, on an Indian.

Clearly, this race puts to rest the long-held myth that Harley-Davidson was not involved in racing in the early years. For already in 1904—the earliest days of its existence—we find Harley-Davidson in the thick of it.

CHAPTER 4

FACTORY EXPANSION AND THE HARLEY-DAVIDSON TWIN

Growth came quickly to the Harley-Davidson Motor Company. In 1906, the woodshed factory turned out about 50 motorcycles. But even tripled in size, and with a drill press and lathe, the woodshed wasn't enough. With an eye toward the future, the founders purchased a lot on Chestnut Street (now Juneau Avenue) and constructed a 20x60-foot wooden building.

With a loan from a Scottish bachelor uncle, bank loans, and the sale of stock after their 1907 incorporation, H-D began to seriously expand. That fall, Bill Harley graduated from college with a degree in mechanical engineering.

Over the winter of 1907–1908, the Juneau Avenue factory received a second story and a general sprucing up. In 1908, a two-story brick addition was added to the building's west side. In 1909, the wooden two-story section was faced

> ## "The buildings of the Harley-Davidson Motor Co. are built to last forever."
> —Meyer Construction Co.'s concrete engineer, 1912

with brick and a 90x120-foot machine shop was added to the factory's east side.

This first substantial Harley-Davidson plant was built of the same buff-colored brick that gave Milwaukee its nickname of "Cream City." It was known to old-timers as the "yellow brick factory."

Company officers believed this facility would be sufficient for several years, but they were wrong. Sales manager Arthur Davidson and his assistant, Albert Becker, recruited new dealers at a dizzying rate. Almost overnight, Harley-Davidson became a force in the marketplace. Production jumped from 150 in 1907 to 3,200 in 1910. Crating was done on the street. Even the old woodshed was pressed back into service.

The Harley-Davidson machine took hold quickly for several reasons. Foremost was the strong demand for a handsome and dependable mount. Advanced over much of the competition when prototyped in 1903, Harley kept ahead of the pack while others stuck to outmoded designs or shoddy construction. There was no radical revision needed, as was the case for Indian in 1909 when that company finally abandoned the bicycle frame.

Changes to the Harley-Davidson were cautious and made only to improve the original pattern.

Looking north on 38th Street toward Chestnut Street (now Juneau Avenue), new construction rises on the site of the yellow brick factory. Unless an early prototype, the bicycle is not a Harley-Davidson, as the Motor Company did not start selling bicycles until 1918 and this photo was taken in 1912. PHOTO COURTESY MILWAUKEE COUNTY HISTORICAL SOCIETY

By early 1911, an addition had been added to the first, five-story, red brick structure built in 1910. To its right, we see Harley's yellow brick factory and attached saw-tooth roof machine shop. In 1912–1913 new buildings would replace these quaint reminders of Harley's early years. *Photo courtesy Milwaukee County Historical Society*

Upgrades came in 1907 with the Sager spring fork; in 1909 with increased displacement of 30.16 cubic inches (495 cc), magneto ignition, hidden controls, and restyled tanks; and in 1910 with an improved belt idler.

Just as vital was Harley-Davidson's commitment to its dealers—nearly 2,000 by 1916. The Milwaukee

As motorcycle production soared, new construction tried to keep pace. This late 1912 view shows the north side of the Harley factory as an addition partly fills in the gap between the 1910–1911 red brick building and the big 1912 "east" addition, barely visible on the far left. By this date, the only remaining segment of the yellow brick factory was the sawtooth machine shop, seen here displaying the large Harley-Davidson name. *Photo courtesy Milwaukee County Historical Society*

Owned by the Harley Archives and on display at the Milwaukee Public Museum, this 1909 twin represents the rarest of the rare. Most writers incorrectly state that the 1909 twin was 49.48 cubic inches (810 cc), but displacement was actually 53.68 cubic inches (880 cc).

"Beehive"-style cylinders made pre-1911 twins unique. Some blamed the 1909 twin's failure on its lack of a belt tensioner, but H-D said the trouble was with the automatic intake valves. When the bike was new it would have run a 28-degree V-belt and not the flat belt shown here.

Chalmer Davidson's nicely restored 1911 magneto-equipped Model 7-C in a rustic setting evokes a less hurried past. By 1911, the Silent Gray Fellow was quickly gaining popularity among American riders.

The gear train on the 1911 magneto model was a major departure from that of earlier battery models. Vertical fins gave 1911 and later motors a different look, although little else had changed.

factory backed its already dependable product with high-quality parts and expert advice. Harley-Davidson president Walter Davidson's "1,000 plus 5" win of the country's premier endurance run in 1908 showed the world Harley-Davidson enthusiasm and durability. With Harley-Davidson, a dealer made both money and friends.

The founders of Harley-Davidson also made the canny decision to grow with the market. In early 1910, they laid the foundation of the modern company by purchasing land west of the yellow brick factory and erecting a new five-story structure of reinforced concrete and red brick.

The new plant was of modern industrial design and contained end walls of removable tiles for future expansion. This came immediately. In November a second red brick addition was authorized. Built on the west side of the new red brick plant, it was finished early in 1911.

Curiously, a story of a hidden room is associated with this second segment of the Juneau Avenue factory. It tells of early bike parts used as backfill behind a wall in the basement. This was told to the author by the late Albert "Squib" Henrich, who in turn heard it from early employee Edwin "Sherbie" Becker in the early 1920s. An attempt in 1992 to find the hidden room proved inconclusive.

Legend aside, production in 1911 zoomed to over 5,600. This included several hundred of the new twin-cylinder models.

America's first V-twin had been marketed by future aviator Glenn Curtiss in 1903 when he introduced a 42.4-cubic-inch (695 cc), 5-horsepower twin. Two years later, in college, Bill Harley began doodling V-twin designs. A second cylinder added to the single was an easy path to more hill-climbing oomph.

Belts had to be kept clean and oiled, and the idler pulley "dropped" at night. When the belt had stretched beyond the limits of idler pulley travel, the rear wheel was moved back and a link added to the pedaling chain.

Owner-builder Bruce Linsday resurrected this 1911 twin around a bare engine. The frame was hand-built, and the rest of the machine is a combination of original and replica parts.

The first Harley-Davidson V-twin prototype was built in late 1906. In February 1907, it was shown at the Chicago motorcycle show. It was rated at 5 horsepower, but displacement and specs are unknown.

There is evidence that a few additional twins were built in 1907 and 1908 as prototypes or racers. A reported 27 twins were built in 1909, and at least one in 1910. The 1909 twin displaced 53.68 cubic inches (880 cc).

To illustrate the rarity of pre-1911 H-D twins, just one example appears in Wisconsin motorcycle registrations before 1911. This was a 7-horsepower 1909 "Model 5-D," registered that spring to H-D engine department foreman Max Kobs.

Everyone else at Harley was still riding singles—including the founders. Not until 1911 were additional twins registered. This was the redesigned 50-cubic-inch (810 cc) Model 7-D. In 1912, a 61-cubic-inch (988 cc) version appeared that soon nudged the smaller twin out of existence.

Harley-Davidson was now on a roll of epic proportions. Output exploded from 9,591 in 1912 to 16,000 in 1914. In 1913, a milestone was

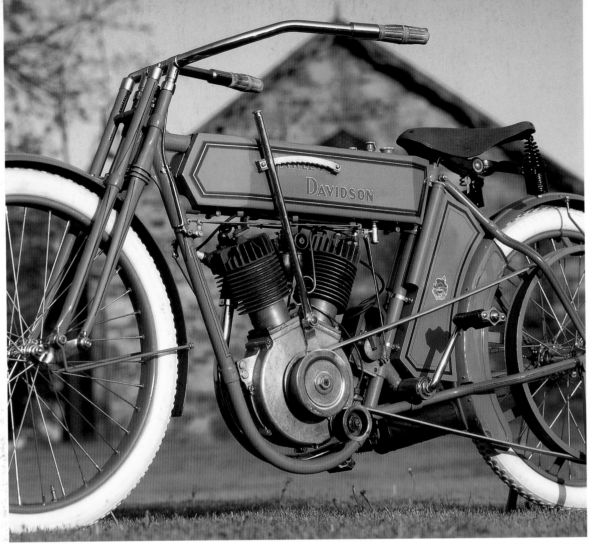

According to Linsday, his early Harley twin isn't much faster than the single, but it goes up hills much better. The V-twin motor fills up the frame nicer too.

reached when more twins than singles were built.

This rapid increase sent Harley-Davidson motorcycles around the globe, a feat made possible by yet more enlargements to the Juneau Avenue plant.

In early 1912, the properties between the yellow brick factory and 37th Street were purchased and the buildings razed. Dynamite broke the frozen ground and Henry Wussow's steam shovel excavated earth that was hauled away by horse-drawn wagons. By May, the Meyer Construction Co. was pouring concrete. Experts were amazed at their speedy progress.

This "east" plant was Harley-Davidson's most ambitious addition during this period. The building was L-shaped to fit the wedge-shaped property and to allow natural light into the structure. Over 700 freight-car loads fed the concrete mixer, and 500,000 pounds of steel reinforcing rod were used. Meyer's crew ("Italian sculptors" Arthur Davidson called them in the Harley-Davidson *Dealer*) mixed, poured, and tamped 28 million pounds of concrete in just 75 days.

On the first of August the top floor was poured

Of his twin's performance, Linsday said, "You can slow down to about 15 miles per hour and then pull the belt tensioner. The belt chirps a couple times and you're off and up to 50 real nice."

Mike Terry's original-condition 1913 single features acetylene lighting, with the acetylene tank mounted on the handlebar. Night riding was a problem in the early days, and many deaths were attributable to hazardous roads and poor lighting.

After singing the praises of automatic intake valves for years, Harley-Davidson went to a mechanically operated intake valve on its single in 1913. This arrangement would remain unchanged until 1930.

Another option in 1913 was the chain-drive single, as shown on this H-D Archives bike at the Milwaukee Public Museum.

What appears to be a rear brake drum on this 1913 single is actually Bill Harley's Free Wheel Control. This modern multi-plate clutch device was a $10 option on both singles and twins. The Free Wheel Control lever is located behind the belt-tensioner lever.

and a Milwaukee German custom observed when a Christmas tree was hoisted aloft. This signaled company president Walter Davidson that Meyer's crew was entitled to free beer.

The east plant added 90,000 square feet of floor space to the factory, thereby doubling the capacity of all previous additions combined. The need for more production space was so great that machinery was installed on a floor as soon as Edward Steigerwald's brick masons closed it in.

But even this wasn't enough room. In September, offices were moved out of the yellow brick factory and a crew razed everything except the sawtooth machine shop. The *Dealer* noted, "The . . . first structure erected on the present site of the Harley-Davidson factory . . . has now passed into history."

With autumn closing in, work on the new addition continued day and night. Arnold Meyer promised "a floor a week" to an anxious Walter Davidson, who held out a $150-per-day bonus for an early finish.

Experts called them crazy for attempting two buildings in one season. As the structure rose, workers in the east building watched the Bar and Shield trademark on the west factory vanish behind

the new construction. Good weather held and the latest addition was occupied as 1913 dawned.

The Motor Company now occupied a factory of nearly 200,000 square feet. With so many new additions, a numbering system was devised, starting with the original woodshed dubbed "factory number 1."

In 1913, the last gap along Juneau Avenue was closed when the 1909 machine shop was razed and was replaced by a six-story plant.

Again, Meyer's crew carried out its duties with precision. The "big bucket" tipped its first load of concrete in May and its last in July. By fall the addition was complete.

Thus, by 1914, Harley-Davidson possessed 300,000 square feet of capacity under one roof. The plant ran along Juneau Avenue for 476 feet. Experts declared the new factory perfect in every respect.

With partition walls removed, the various segments merged into a single facility as workers moved freely throughout the plant. The identities of additions Nos. 3, 4, 5, 6, and 8—along with the now vanished yellow brick factory—were soon forgotten.

The original woodshed was brought to the Juneau Avenue factory where it stood for decades as a reflection of the past. For in ten years' time a backyard operation had been transformed into a world-famous company.

The founders looked confidently toward the future, but other forces were at work: forces that would threaten everyone's lofty predictions.

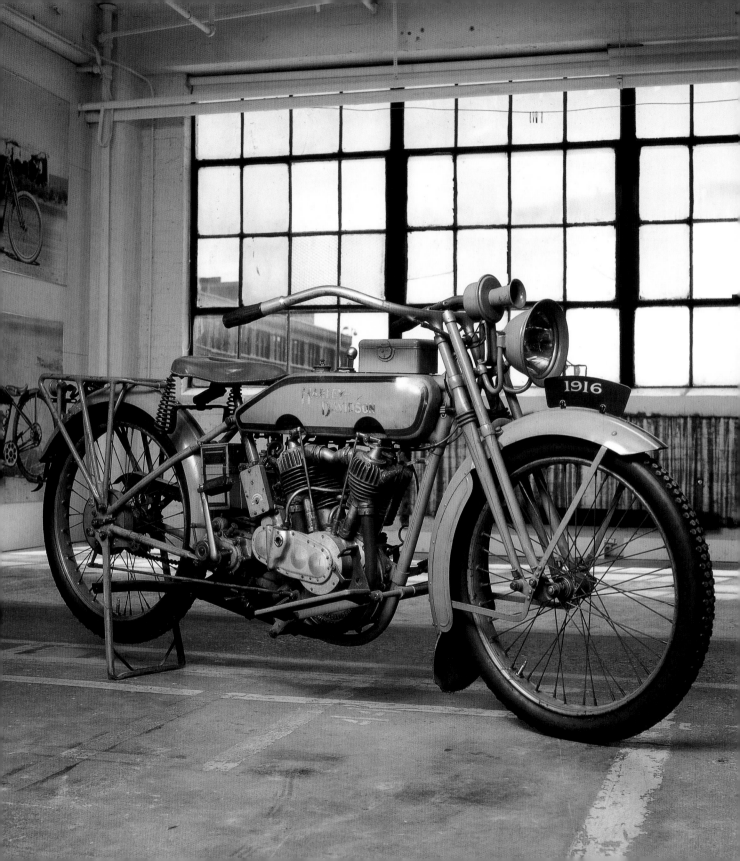

CHAPTER 5
THE
FIGHTING MOTORCYCLE

World War I devastated the original U.S. motorcycle industry. In 1914, there were nearly two dozen factories turning out heavyweight V-twin motorcycles. Rising wages and prices, scarcity of components, and better profits elsewhere killed off the majority of builders. When the dust settled in 1919 you could count the survivors on one hand. But if the war wrecked the smaller concerns, it helped Harley-Davidson.

The U.S. Army first tested motorcycles in 1908, but found the iron horse wanting compared to the four-legged variety. By the time of World War I, however, the Harley-Davidson had grown up, as evidenced by the chart on page 40.

While the Harley-Davidson motorcycle of 1916 was a world apart from the 1905 model, an unbroken design continuity lay between these machines. Just as Bill Harley had "growed" the single into a twin by grafting on a second cylinder, further improvements were made in step-by-step increments until 1916 when the classic American motorcycle layout stabilized. It remained unchanged for the next 33 years.

By 1914, the War Department was testing motorcycles again, inspired this time by the mechanization of European armies. During World War I, the British Army alone used 70,000 bikes. A new and unexpected use for the motorcycle had come into being: warfare.

Technically neutral until 1917, the U.S. Army had no battleground experience with the motorcycle until 1916. Then trouble developed along the Mexican border with Pancho Villa's revolutionary army. This gave Harley-Davidson an excuse for taking the motorcycle into the fight.

Some National Guard units had already formed motorcycle companies. One Illinois H-D dealer was begging the government for machine guns so his riders could act as "light artillery." Wanting something official, the U.S. Army invited Bill Harley to the Springfield Armory where he helped develop the "fighting motorcycle."

The military had high hopes for the new weapon. Unlike the mule-packed machine gun that took several minutes to unload and set up, the sidecar machine gun was available within seconds. Some claimed a single machine-gun-equipped sidecar equaled 1,000 riflemen in firepower!

> ## "This is no place for a timid person like me."
> —Arthur Davidson on the Mexican border, 1916

This 1916 twin located in H-D Archives, shows the great advance the Silent Gray Fellow made in 10 years' time. This is the bike H-D took to war. Building seen through window is the "Factory No. 5" portion of the Juneau Avenue complex built in 1912.

With the adoption of the kickstarter in 1916, the modern H-D layout stabilized. In 1915, they had a three-speed transmission but with "step" starting, and in 1914, a two-speed rear hub with pedal starting. Before that, it was all single-speed.

1905 H-D, Single Cylinder
Displacement: 26.84 cubic inches (440 cc)
Output: 3 1/4 horsepower
Ignition: coil/dry-cell battery
Lubrication: drip feed
Suspension: front: rigid, rear: seat springs
Transmission: none (single speed)
Starting: jump on/no clutch
Wheelbase: 51 inches
Tires: 2 1/4 inches
Final drive: flat belt
Weight: 138 pounds
Lighting: none
Top speed: 50 miles per hour (racing pulley)

1916 H-D, Twin Cylinder
Displacement: 60.34 cubic inches (988.83 cc)
Output: 11 horsepower
Ignition: magneto or generator-battery
Lubrication: pressurized feed-pump plus
    auxiliary handpump
Suspension: front: spring fork, rear: Ful-Floteing
    seat-post plus seat springs
Transmission: three-speed
Starting: kickstarter with clutch
Wheelbase: 59 1/2 inches
Tires: 3 inches
Final drive: chain
Weight: 325 pounds
Lighting: electric on Model 16-J
Top speed: 70 miles per hour

The fighting motorcycle was tested near Milwaukee, in deep mud, early in 1916. Firing at ranges between 250 and 500 yards, it satisfied military and factory observers. Afterwards, these machines were shipped to New Mexico for service along the border.

Propaganda dispatches from England portrayed the military motorcyclist as a romantic figure dodging mortar shells and machine gun fire. Riders were shown aiming a pistol in one direction while heading in another—a practice not conducive to longevity.

Early reports from Mexico told similar tales. One extolled Private Gregg of the U.S. Seventh Cavalry, who rode his Harley-Davidson through a gang of banditos with his .45 Colt semi-automatic pistol blazing, killing one, wounding another, then delivering his dispatch case safely at headquarters.

While such exciting events no doubt took place, the truth was closer to the report of one newspaper correspondent who wrote: "A motorcycle coughed past, chasing runaway mules through the mesquite."

Used against a lightly armed adversary on foot or horseback in the open Southwest, the machine-gun sidecar was probably fairly effective. Even so, hidden opponents armed with the accurate, clip-fed Mexican Mauser rifle could wreak havoc on a target as big as a sidecar.

Harley-Davidson's fighting motorcycle was tested in the spring of 1916 at a rifle range near the Racine-Milwaukee county line. Clay mud encountered en route forced the removal of the front fenders. After posing for photographers and being cleaned up at the factory, these machines were shipped to the Mexican border for active duty. PHOTO COURTESY MILWAUKEE COUNTY HISTORICAL SOCIETY

One thing quickly learned was the need to adequately train motorcyclist soldiers. Studies showed that 90 percent of a motorcycle's efficiency depended on the rider and mechanic and only 10 percent on the machine.

Badly trained conscripts were accident prone, and poorly maintained machines subject to breakdown. This moved the Milwaukee factory to send out instructors for training rider-soldiers and mechanics. A school at the factory was set up by service department head Joe Kilbert in 1917. Howard "Hap" Jameson was the first instructor. The service school exists to the present day.

Based on experience in Mexico, the Army forged ahead with the fighting motorcycle once officially engaged in the European conflict. Experts forecasted 20,000 motorcycles for every million soldiers in the trenches.

The reality of modern warfare, however, was far different from skirmishing in Mexico. Bad ground, bottomless mud, shattered roads, endless debris, booby traps, and vulnerability to return fire restricted the military motorcycle to rear-echelon service.

Here the motorcycle—usually with sidecar—did quite well for dispatch work, convoy control, military police, supply needs, communications repair, medic duty, and other auxiliary uses.

Still, wartime conditions demanded great durability. Even taking into account the self-congratulatory approach that Harley-Davidson was so good at, it appears that American machines stood up better in warfare than did English and French bikes—with Harleys doing best of all.

A special magazine—Harley-Davidson Folks—was published for servicemen. In late 1917, one soldier wrote to this publication: "for real comedy you ought to see . . . these French machines . . . so many levers and controls on them they look more like a linotype machine. . . . I actually had the nerve to . . . ride one, but got the spark to exploding in the transmission case and the exhaust snorted into the magneto and quit."

One Harley-Davidson reportedly took part in the Mexican border ruckus, then served in France on "16,000 miles of as rough a run as pneumatic tires have ever turned upon or engine pumped across."

This reputation led to the selection of William S. Harley as head of the Society of Automotive

Machine gun–equipped Harleys were given a thorough workout in the Southwest desert in 1916 as a prelude to their use in Europe. While shown here as mobile units of war able to run rings around an opponent, the combat role of the motorcycle turned out to be very limited. PHOTO COURTESY MILWAUKEE COUNTY HISTORICAL SOCIETY

This Milwaukee street scene was photographed shortly after America's entry into World War I. It suggests a Harley-Davidson rider has dismounted to hear the patriotic speech of an army recruiter. In total, 312 Harley-Davidson employees served in the armed forces. Three were killed. *PHOTO COURTESY MILWAUKEE COUNTY HISTORICAL SOCIETY*

Engineers' committee on standardized military motorcycles. Committee members came from the ranks of American motorcycle builders. Their work resulted in the "Liberty Motorcycle," a standardized machine based on the best features of various civilian types.

Harley-Davidson's major contributions included engine, wheels, and controls. Prototypes were built and tested in 1918, but the war ended before production began.

During the war, 312 employees from Harley-Davidson served in the armed forces. Three were killed in action.

Because Milwaukee was heavily German, American patriotism was serious business in Beer City. The bronze statue goddess *Germania* was cut up for scrap. A legend in the Harley family tells of government agents watching the house during the war because Bill Harley's wife, Anna, was of German descent. On the day of the armistice, Harley-Davidson employees led the victory parade downtown.

The war boosted Harley-Davidson in several ways. Unlike Indian, who early-on took big military contracts, the Milwaukee factory did not commit to full war production until very late. Dealers could get bikes and parts from Harley all through the war except for a six-month period in 1918.

As a result, disgruntled Indian riders and orphans from the many now-defunct makes swelled Harley's ranks. Harley-Davidson could brag about not diverting production into the foreign military market as Indian had—thus portraying Milwaukee as the rider's friend.

World War I gained Harley-Davidson a worldwide reputation for durability. In 1990, the late William H. Davidson told me, "Harley got its deepest breath over in the mud in France. . . . After World War I we went ahead of Indian and stayed ahead forever."

The greatest tribute to the Harley-Davidson motorcycle came after the war when surplus machines were sold at auction. After the new, still-in-the-crate

This 1919 J model, owned by John Vandenover, is similar to WWI Army bikes. Even the paint color is the same, although tank graphics on military bikes were less flamboyant.

Harleys were purchased, bidding agents from foreign governments announced they would buy *used* Harley-Davidsons before buying new machines from other manufacturers.

Stories of World War I military Harleys still surface. One old-time Wisconsin rider, Alfred Embretsen, told me a story of a guy doing back-hoe work years ago at Camp McCoy, where in 1917 the Milwaukee Motorcycle Ambulance Co. No. 1 was stationed.

"He dug up an entire row of World War I Harleys." Embretsen said. "Some were still in the crates. There were horse saddles and other equipment too. When he asked if he could salvage them, the officer in charge hollered. 'Nothing doing! Go back out there and bury them right back up.'"

CHAPTER 6
THE
GANG'S ALL HERE

After World War I the American motorcycling landscape was drastically altered. Great names had vanished forever. Indian now occupied second place, and Ignaz Schwinn's Excelsior-Henderson brought up the rear.

Milwaukee was on top.

At Harley-Davidson the old guard was firmly in place. Founders William S. Harley, Arthur Davidson, Walter Davidson, and William A. Davidson were now in their prime.

Several top men had followed Bill Davidson from the railshops, including plant supervisor George Nortman. Other valuable employees had come from the Thor and Feilbach motorcycle companies.

An efficient office and sales staff; experienced engineering, experimental, and racing departments; and hundreds of skilled machinists and laborers rounded out the work force at Harley-Davidson.

Although Clifford Pease's restored 1922 JD model is not completely authentic, it's still a good example of an early 74-cubic-inch Harley F-head. By 1922, Ford's Model T had dropped below the Harley Big Twin in price.

which totaled 2,350 people in a company that had done $14 million of business in 1919 dollars.

With the prewar competition weeded out and greater dealer and rider loyalty in place, the good times seemed ready to roll. Once again, Harley-Davidson expanded. In 1919, the new "south" complex at Juneau Avenue was begun. Factory floor space again doubled, with production capacity rising to 35,000 motorcycles per year—a figure the founders would never see reached.

The peak year for the American motorcycle industry was 1913. As shown, the war was a double-edged sword—helping Harley-Davidson but knocking out many smaller outfits. After 1920, however, even Milwaukee was feeling pain, no matter how hard they tried to ignore it. This reversal in fortunes was largely due to Henry Ford's Model T.

Reliable and cheap to begin with, the Model T just kept getting cheaper. By the 1920s the motorcycle's early popularity had vanished. The time when doctors used two-wheelers for house calls was gone forever.

The motorcycle's early price advantage was also gone. A cost comparison between Harley's V-twin

"For the rider who simply must have the fastest thing on wheels."
—Two-Cam sales literature, 1928

and Ford's Model T illustrates the throat-slashing competition the motorcycle faced:

Harley-Davidson (Twin)	Ford Model T (Runabout)
1909 (54 ci) $325	1909 $825
1913 (61 ci) $350	1913 $525
1916 (61 ci) $295	1916 $345
1920 (61 ci) $395	1920 (March) $550 (Sept.) $395
1922 (74 ci) $390	1922 $319
1925 (74 ci) $335	1925 $260

Ford's downward pressure on the price of transportation was crushing. After 1920, Ford's cheapest car actually dropped *below* Harley's V-twin in price. Historians who beat the tom-tom of an "Indian vs. Harley" war have it wrong. That was nothing but a sideshow to excite the riders. Behind the scenes, Harley-Davidson, "Pop" Schwinn, and Indian worked together. They knew the real enemy—Henry Ford.

Without the economy of scale that Ford possessed, no motorcycle factory could compete on a price basis. At the 1920 dealers' convention, a bitter Walter Davidson said, "Henry Ford is given credit for the price decline [but] he simply is a victim of circumstances. . . . His car will carry you over the road, but has none of the qualifications that a modern car has."

This was whistling in the graveyard, and Walter knew it. The motorcycle was in deep trouble. The Ford wasn't fancy, but as basic transportation it had more "qualifications" than any motorcycle. To approximate an automobile you needed a sidecar, and that cost another hundred bucks.

Attempting to broaden the motorcycle's appeal, Harley-Davidson introduced the "Sport Model" (Model W) in 1919. This 35.64-cubic-inch (584 cc) "flat twin" showed some advanced and original features. If patents granted to Bill Harley are any indication, Milwaukee had big plans for it.

It's tempting to say that the Sport Model was intended to be a two-wheeled Model T. It weighed a hundred pounds less than the V-twin, and, with its low center of gravity, was a sweet handling mount. Its opposed-cylinder engine was sewing-machine smooth, and with gear primary-drive and enclosed rear chain it was quiet, clean, and efficient.

In theory, the public should have flocked to the Sport, but like most smaller motorcycles that appeared in the post–World War I period, it failed. Price was one barrier—$325 in 1919. There was also the Sport's unorthodox appearance, which damned it in the eyes of V-twin–loving Americans. Weak performance was another nail in the Sport's coffin. After five years it faded away, leaving the 61-cubic-inch V-twin to carry the torch, along with the 74-cubic-inch "Superpowered Twin" that appeared in 1921.

Intended for sidecar and high-speed solo work, the 74 was a 61 that had been bored and stroked

Standard J-series engine used a single camshaft with cam followers that severely limited rpm, but that was not so important in an age of poor roads and 30-mile-per-hour speed limits.

Harley's Sport Model was unorthodox with its opposed horizontal cylinders and external flywheel. Almost nothing on it followed standard Harley practice. Bob McClean own's this nice 1922 example.

to 3 7/16x4 inches. Harley-Davidson knew its customers' tastes when advertising that. "If you want to enjoy the feel and thrill of piloting a motorcycle of extra mighty power, get a Harley-Davidson 74 Superpowered Twin Motorcycle."

From the beginning the motorcycle had been defined by speed and power, but that too came back to haunt Harley-Davidson. Because if Milwaukee wasn't busy enough fighting the cheap automobile, there was another problem to battle: the public's hatred for two-wheelers.

Guess again if you think the "bad boy" image started with *The Wild One*. In the beginning the masses despised *all* motor vehicles. But while the automobile became acceptable, the motorcycle industry nearly committed *hara-kiri* by exploiting the two-wheeler's most troubling aspect: sudden death.

The Sport Model engine was Harley's first side-valve. Transmission was positioned over the engine. Note the combined intake and exhaust manifolds.

The emphasis on speed racing came from the motorcycle's bicycle roots. The biggest early racing promoter was a former bicycle racing champ— Indian founder George Hendee.

Hendee used the Indian motorcycle like a war club. He encouraged dealers to race and sent factory teams on the warpath to scalp the competition. Under Hendee, Indian reigned supreme.

In the day of the single-cylinder this didn't mean much, but with the rise of the V-twin and track speeds of 100 miles per hour by 1912 on the wooden-banked motordromes, the motorcycle's homicidal soul was released.

Board-track racing was dubbed the "craziest sport in the world" by newspapers, which decorated motordrome articles with grim reapers and winged death's heads. Outraged by the infernal racket of unmuffled engines and the aura of violent death, the public labeled them "murder-dromes" and civic do-gooders demanded their abolition.

Harley-Davidson long resisted this racing trend. Their motorcycle was of a practical nature—

Harley's Eight-Valve racer bested Indian in the 1910s and 1920s, but professional racing, with its many deaths and injuries, put a black mark on the sport of motorcycling. John Paeham's excellent 1928 model was "built" by Mike Lange.

Close-up of a 1927 Eight-Valve engine shows the large dual exhaust ports and multi-valve arrangement. This was Harley's only four-valve-per-head engine until the VR1000 factory racer appeared in 1994. Motor courtesy R. L. Jones.

The Harley F-head went out in a blaze of glory with the 1928 Two-Cam road model. Acceleration was brisk with a top solo speed of about 80 to 85 miles per hour. Mike Terry owns this nice 74-cubic-inch JDH.

a dependable pleasure mount where high speed was not an end in itself. For the first decade this formula proved successful. When the factory competed they favored endurance and reliability events, and except for a few attempts early on, shied away from pure speed.

This changed in 1912 when a motordrome was built in Milwaukee. The roar of racing victories could be heard all over town, but none went to the home factory. The laughing Indian appeared on billboards and everybody knew the butt of the joke: Harley-Davidson.

Enough was enough. In 1913, Harley-Davidson enticed racing boss William Ottaway away from Thor—the god of thunder. Of Ottaway, the late William H. Davidson said, "[He] developed the first Eight-Valve and the standard pocket-valve [racers]. . . . He got those so they would sing . . . a fine mechanical wizard."

After a mediocre start in 1914, the Harley-Davidson factory team—soon dubbed the "wrecking crew"—took sweeping victories at Dodge City and other prestigious events. With the famous Two-Cam and Eight-Valve racers, Harley-Davidson smashed Indian's former dominance into pieces that the once-proud "Wigwam" could never put back together again.

But speed racing came with a heavy price. Advertising manager Walter Kleimenhagen told dealers, "racing—that magic form of advertising . . . it's great . . . but land sakes how it costs."

The price went beyond dollars and cents. It gave the motorcycle a deadly image and stereotyped the rider as an antisocial speed freak—a maniac dashing from place to place with throttle and cutout wide open, spilling his guts over the landscape in the process.

It's ironic that today, an important part of Harley-Davidson marketing is based on a "bad boy" image, because for much of the company's history such an idea was taboo. Yet the founders themselves were responsible for this state of affairs when they turned their plow horse into a racing stud.

In 1928, they caved in to this lust for speed by offering the previously competition-only Two-Cam engine in road-bike form. These were the famous JH (61-cubic-inch) and JDH (74-cubic-inch) models. At the time, these bikes were the fastest stock Harleys ever offered and among the fastest vehicles on the road. In one ad a factory oracle said, "The magic words 'two cam' mean exceptional speed and tremendous power."

This shows how schizophrenic Harley-Davidson could be. Time and again they'd swear off racing and decry speed, but then like addicts they'd come crawling back to the race track or encourage road riders with the Two-Cam. In 1929, you could even special order an 80-cubic-inch Two-Cammer!

Together these poisoned apple factors removed the American motorcycle from mainstream transportation into a suspect, cult-like status. Throughout the 1920s, H-D operated at about half capacity. Export, commercial, and law enforcement sales kept the factory alive, but the motorcycle found itself in dark waters, with civic reformers asking why it should exist at all.

Front wheel brake first appeared in 1928 and wasn't the dangerous device many thought. By the late 1920s, however, the Big Twin was taking on an antiquated look. Few significant changes had taken place for several years.

55

CHAPTER 7

SINGLES FOR THE MASSES

But speed was just one card in Harley's deck. More typically, the company portrayed the sidecar as an elegant alternative to the automobile. Colorful ads showed finely coiffured ladies disembarking at theaters or restaurants.

Another tactic had overseas origins. From their "London branch." H-D's founders were familiar with the English bike scene. They marveled at the clean reputation motorcycles possessed in Great Britain. where all ages and classes rode.

This inspired Harley's "good rider" campaign. Ads offered "English serge" outfits. and slogans such as "Natty Suits for Neat Riders." During the 1920s. British tweeds were high motorcycle fashion. Accessory manager Hugh Sharp commented to dealers in 1920. "The sight of the white-collared chap with . . . neat fitting clothing and quiet running motorcycle is a creator of envy . . . instead of being a disturber of mental machinery."

"The overhead Singles were not without friends."
—New York Motorcycle Show, 1928

The 1926 Model B was Harley's first 21-cubic-inch Single. This machine was a test bed for several new features and developed into the side-valve twins. Its spring fork is similar to that used on the 1936 Knucklehead. Owned by Don Huffman and Greg Taylor.

In 1926, attempting to create a more socially acceptable bike that would also appeal to the export market. Harley-Davidson introduced a new machine: the Model B 21-cubic-inch Single.

With 2 7/8 x 3 1/4-inch bore and stroke, the new Single displaced just 21.09 cubic inches (350 cc). It was the smallest Harley-Davidson to date—smaller than the original 405 cc 1903 bike.

Taking into account their experience with the innovative but unconventional Sport Model, H-D built the new Single along traditional lines. In the United States it was aimed at riders intimidated by the Big Twin. and also provided a low-cost alternative to the automobile.

Overseas. where gasoline prices were higher. the factory hoped that the Single's great economy. along with Harley-Davidson reliability. would translate into big sales—and profits.

Tipping the scales at around 260 pounds. the new Single was no lightweight. Hap Jameson said in the *Enthusiast*. "When my turn came to try out this new member of the family I kinda felt like I had been asked to go strolling a baby cart. But. that little boat is no baby cart—no siree."

The 21 Single is usually lost in the stampede of V-twins. when in truth it was a landmark bike because with it. Bill Harley was mapping the future.

Using a twin-cam layout, the new Single was a smaller motorcycle with a big-bike ancestry and look. It ran full-sized footboards, a pressurized oil system, and a three-speed transmission. Electrics were the same as the Big Twin's. "Just like its papa," Hap boasted proudly, handing out verbal cigars to potential buyers.

The fork was new, and similar in style to 1936-and-later springers. The frame was a lighter version of the Big Twin's with the same spring seatpost. "No jolting . . . your gold fillings when you ride this baby," Hap promised.

Balloon tires improved the ride even more. "Hot puppies," Hap exclaimed. "These big rubber doughnuts are comfort producers."

Styling of the new Single followed the "streamline" look that first appeared on 1925 Big

The 21 Single was dubbed an "80 miles per gallon" bike due to great economy of operation.

Both the 45 and the Sportster inherited their right-side drive chain position from the 21 Single. The bearing bosses for the two camshafts are clearly evident from embossing on cover. The first 45 was this bike with a second cylinder and two more cams thrown in.

Twins. With shapely tanks and a lower frame, the modern Harley look was ushered in.

But the real significance of the Single was its existence in two similar, yet radically different, forms. You might call them rival fraternal twins because the Model "B" had a side-valve engine, while the Model BA had an overhead-valve engine.

The side-valve Single was no great shakes. That engine type had been championed by Indian for years and Harley had used it in the Sport Model. But the BA—the 21 OHV Single—was another story.

Except for professional Eight-Valve overhead racers, Harley riders had never seen an overhead-valve engine come out of Milwaukee. Now they had one in road-bike form—if only a single.

Already in the 1910s, riders knew that putting overhead valves in the gasoline engine was a kick-ass

With front stand and foot pegs, this 21 OHV at the AMA's Motorcycle Heritage Museum is set up like an export model. Dual headlights are probably not original.

combination. It was still heady stuff in 1926 when the BA hit the street with its pushrod-activated valves opening into a hemispherical-shaped combustion chamber. This was the kind of technology you'd find in high-performance aircraft engines.

Logically, Harley-Davidson should have trumpeted the BA's superior overhead-valve technology from the lofty ramparts of Juneau Avenue. Curiously, they did not. Milwaukee was strangely silent about the 21 OHV. When presenting the 1926 line in the *Enthusiast*, the 21 OHV version was missing—an eerie foreshadowing of the 61 OHV's stealth introduction 10 years later.

Harley-Davidson probably chose not to push the 21 OHV because H-D's next generation of V-twins were all going to be side-valves. The first, the 45-cubic-inch (2 3/4x3 13/16-inch bore and stroke) Model D V-twin was introduced in 1929. The D was little more than the side-valve 21 Single

The 21 OHV was a small masterpiece of overhead-valve engineering. Combustion chamber shape and rocker arm design would find their way into the legendary Knuckle-head engine.

Thus, it wouldn't pay to sing hosannas to the overhead-valve Single when the new twins were all side-valves. The 21 OHV was like Cinderella locked in the attic while her side-valve sisters were portrayed as technological beauty queens with their "famous Ricardo Combustion Heads."

That was true—sort of. Harry Ricardo had breathed new life into the side-valve engine by redesigning the shape of the combustion chamber. This permitted higher compression with less chance of detonation. ("Whew!" Hap groaned in the *Enthusiast*. "I wish engineers would use words that mean something to me.")

with a second cylinder and two more cams incorporated into the motor. At first the 45 and 21 even shared frame and transmission.

In 1930, the new Model VL 74-cubic-inch side-valve Big Twin joined the lineup. Harley bragged that the VL was essentially an enlarged 45 twin. Not very exciting stuff. Lots of guys stuck with their Two-Cams.

Economics probably tipped Harley's hand. Cheap to build, the side-valve would pay the bills. In the automobile industry, the side-valve engine dominated; Harley-Davidson was just joining the party.

But there were plenty of people around Harley-Davidson who considered the side-valve to be Indian's motor and hated it. Alfred Feldmann, then in H-D's engineering department, later recalled of the side-valve in Maurice Hendry's 1972 book *Harley-Davidson*, "I was never in favor of that valve arrangement in an air-cooled engine."

The 45-cubic-inch side-valve engine appeared in 1929 as an answer to the Super X and Indian Scout. Note that each valve has its own camshaft and a very straight valve angle. Bob and Patti Studer own this 1932 Servi-Car.

The VL side-valve 74-cubic-inch engine replaced the F-head in the Big Twin line in 1930. It was little more than an enlarged 45. The Bluegrass Motorcycle Museum in Kentucky owns this handsome example.

While the side-valve engine was a cleaner design than its F-head predecessors, road conditions and rider expectations were racing ahead of the performance the VL could deliver.

good production start of 8,000 in 1926, numbers started falling off. This decline was largely the result of Harley's export market drying up due to a stiff rise in British tariff rates throughout the "sterling bloc."

In this country, H-D made the mistake of targeting the Single to automobile drivers when the real market was boys and teenagers. One critic wrote to Arthur Davidson in 1927, "I am for the motorcyclist and not for the automobile owner." Under these circumstances the poor little Single never had a chance.

Yet all was not lost. In 1925, the American Motorcycle Association (AMA) sanctioned a new 21.35-cubic-inch racing class. The inaugural race was held in Milwaukee with a crowd of 20,000 watching Eddie Brinck, Jim Davis, and Joe Petrali sling their wicked little Singles around the track, cracking 80 miles per hour on the straight. This was the dawn of Harley's famous "Peashooter."

Anyone wandering down for a look at the racing bikes quickly had their eyes opened. For all the Peashooters had overhead-valve engines—a high performance version of the 21 OHV road bike.

As a result, most 21 Singles were side-valves. This was the famous "80 miles per gallon" bike, so cheap to run it would have pleased the Scots "honey uncle." As Hap promised, "The hinges on your old pocket book will rust from non-use if you buy gas for this buggy."

At last Harley-Davidson had a Model T on two wheels. The Single was cheaper to operate than an auto (1 cent per mile vs. 7 cents), cheaper than streetcar fare, and easy to park. The Single was billed as the new way to "power travel" that you could purchase with easy "Pay As You Ride" terms.

The 21 Single even undercut Ford's cheapest car by $150; trouble was, nobody much cared anymore. Used autos glutted the market. After a

The VL was an interesting bike during a transition period in Harley history. While reminiscent of earlier bikes in many ways, the VL was a more substantial machine. Hand oil pump is visible just behind left-hand filler caps.

Competition 21 Singles were overhead-valve, as shown on this 1926 example owned by Bruce Linsday. These little bikes could easily crack 80 miles per hour.

The overhead-valve Peashooter gave Harley lots of valuable experience on the racetrack. This was Harley's first engine with a hemispherical combustion chamber.

Word soon leaked out. Even the editor of the *Enthusiast* (as politically correct then as now) cryptically remarked. "The old timers. the vet riders after witnessing these 21 cubic inch races agreed that the future of motorcycle racing in America depends largely upon them."

For no matter how much brag was given to genuine Ricardo heads or 80 miles-per-gallon. astute parties could see the 21 OHV was a hot little number. The Peashooter was Harley's bright spot on the racetrack during the late 1920s and showed the way ahead. From this small beginning. the words "overhead-valve" soon became a mantra for performance-minded riders.

Yet anyone wishing for an overhead-valve twin from Milwaukee was greatly disappointed with the new 45- and 74-cubic-inch side-valve twins. An overhead-valve road twin from Harley-Davidson probably seemed as far away as the moon.

CHAPTER 8

HOME-BREW
AND FACTORY 45 OHVs

In reality, new Harley-Davidson overhead-valve twins were not far away, but when they appeared in 1927 they weren't factory jobs, but radical homebuilt hillclimbers.

By the mid-1920s, the hillclimber had eclipsed the motorcycle speed artist. As the club scene grew under the auspices of the AMA, so did slant shooting. All a club needed was a steep country slope where roaring motorcycles weren't a social contagion.

Professional riders ruled the slant. Factory or dealer provided a hillclimb bike, mechanic, and travel expenses. The rider provided the skill and kept the winnings. Slant artists were considered *real* men and were popular with the ladies.

The engine in this hillclimber is the 1928 hybrid Two-Cam/OHV. It has a JDH bottom end, Peashooter heads, and special cast cylinders. The bike is owned by the Motorcycle Heritage Museum and is on display at the Motorsports Hall of Fame Museum.

"It's a pleasure to see Art ride but the girls get a bigger 'goose flesh' out of his 'smile.' These motorcycle boys DO get 'em."
—The Harley-Davidson Enthusiast

Although hillclimbing was rough and tumble, serious injuries were rare. Image-sensitive Harley-Davidson liked that. But winning was everything, and while H-D's 61- and 80-cubic-inch F-head hillclimbers were competitive in the larger displacement events, Milwaukee was caught short in the hot new 45-cubic-inch class.

Back in 1925, Chicago-based Excelsior-Henderson threw a wild card into the mix with their new 45-cubic-inch Super X twin. This F-head sported advanced features, which included gear primary-drive and strong unit construction.

In this trend toward smaller, higher performance motorcycles, the 45 class quickly became an arena for the pros. On the Super X, Joe Petrali and Gene Rhyne reclaimed Excelsior's early glory by winning several hillclimb championships.

Indian countered the Super X threat by enlarging its Scout to 45 cubic inches in 1927, and later dished out more-potent 45 OHV hillclimbers. Until

1929. Harley-Davidson was the underdog in the 45 class. Without a 45-cubic-inch hillclimber, Harley riders played catch up as they hollered at Milwaukee for help.

Significantly, the 21 OHV Single was sometimes effective in battling Super X and Indian 45s.

It happened in 1926, when Herb Reiber's win at Slinger, Wisconsin, allowed the *Enthusiast* to crow, "The . . . Single slipped a fast one over when it assailed the slant in the 45 . . . Event, leaving the twins to take second and third. Wow! A Single beats twins!"

Motor in the Two-Cam/OHV was done so professionally by H-D's experimental and racing departments that it's difficult to see it's actually two engines combined into one. Until now, the Two-Cam/OHV's key role in Harley history has been overlooked.

The business end of the Two-Cam/OHV shows the reason for an overhead-valve hillclimb twin. Torque and high revs of this experimental 45 OHV provided a temporary solution in 1928 against Super X and Indian in the 45-cubic-inch class.

"made from two overhead-valve Singles." The Camel was good enough for Lenz to take some firsts in 1927 and 1928. The bike still exists.

Lenz's home-built 45 OHV Harley wasn't the only one active in 1927. In July, one observer noted a "new design Harley 42 [*sic*] cubic inch motor" built by Ralph Moore of Indianapolis. He added. "No. we did not hit the bottle or pick up a pipe before we wrote that last line. It is a fact. Moore took a 61 Harley. junked most of the motor except the cases, and constructed a 42 cubic inch Harley, using the cylinders and pistons from two 21 cubic inch O. V. Single Harleys."

Such David vs. Goliath victories were rare. and confined to hills that didn't need the chains and dig-out power necessary in loose dirt. But they made Harley riders gaze fondly at the high-revving Peashooter engine to see where the answer lay: overhead-valves.

Over the winter of 1926–1927. two enterprising Harley-Davidson dealers created 45 OHVs. These "Home-Brews" (named after a favorite Prohibition beverage) first appeared in June 1927. at a Lansing. Michigan. climb when Jack Pine enduro winner Oscar Lenz fielded a bike that *MotorCycling* described as a "45 cubic inch Harley" and onlookers dubbed "the Camel."

Lenz's Harley 45 was built on a 1925 61-cubic-inch Two-Cam bottom end with a top end

The frame on the Two-Cam/OHV appears to be from a later DAH factory hillclimber. The single-exhaust-port head differs from two other known Two-Cam/OHVs which have two-port heads, showing that Harley was experimenting.

This "built" 1930 DAH factory hillclimber was crafted by R. L. Jones. Hillclimber styling was the original inspiration for "bobber" and "chopper" road bikes. Note the original chopper-esque fuel tank and cool trailing-link fork.

Noting the success of the Lenz and Moore Home-Brews, Milwaukee created its own 45 OHV in 1928. Whether the impetus came from the Harley factory or Bill Knuth's nearby Milwaukee dealership isn't clear. Knuth promoted professional hillclimbing heavily, and was a factory pet. Although Harley was working on a totally new 45 OHV hillclimber (the 4-camshaft DAH), the factory had good reason to help Knuth. The DAH wouldn't be ready until 1929, and the pros were crying for a 45 OHV for the 1928 season.

Because the 1928 45 OHV hillclimber was not catalogued, determining the bike's origin is difficult. Documentation was lost when Harley-Davidson purged old records, after Bill Knuth's death in 1959.

It's unclear whether these experimental overheads were constructed at the factory or at Knuth's dealership. But if built by Knuth, there was certainly critical factory help. Old-timers remember Harley's experimental and racing departments giving "our Bill" anything he wanted.

Three of these unique 45 OHV hillclimbers survive. All are built on 1928 or 1929 FH or JDH Two-Cam crankcases and show evidence of being constructed by the same hands. Information from the Motorcycle Heritage Museum tells that paid-factory-hillclimber and assistant-service-school-instructor Herb Reiber reworked patterns for the 21 Single cylinder from which six pairs of new cylinders were cast to fit the bigger Two-Cam bottom end.

Due to the excellent workmanship evident on the surviving engines, it's likely that Harley's experimental department reworked the 21 OHV heads to make front and rear cylinders for a twin. Antique bike restorer Mike Lange, who worked on one of these hybrid motors, said this about the cylinder head modifications he noted: "The intake manifold was done up very professionally with a nickel (welding) rod. . . . Along with the cylinders it's my opinion that these were done at the factory."

The DAH was H-D's first regular production OHV hillclimber. The motor was also used in export road racers. Ordinary riders wouldn't see a motor in this class until the 1957 Sportster.

The parent 61 motor's 3 1/2-inch stroke was retained while the bore was changed to 2 7/8 inches using the Dow metal Peashooter piston. This gave an engine of 45.44 cubic inches (744.6 cc) displacement. The resulting motor had the direct-cam action and strong internals of the Two-Cam racer with the breathing advantages of overhead-valves. By a quirk of fate, this experimental and largely forgotten 45 OHV hillclimber may have inspired the greatest motorcycle of them all: the Knucklehead.

The first appearance of Milwaukee's Two-Cam/OHV came in May of 1928—a full year before historians say H-D fielded a 45 OHV hillclimber. It was ridden at Fond du Lac, Wisconsin, by Art Earlenbaugh, who worked at Bill Knuth's dealership and later in H-D's experimental department. Correspondent Hap Jameson commented,

Redesigned Peashooter heads led to the DAH pattern. During the late 1920s and early 1930s, H-D experimented with OHV technology. One entire bike—the 1929 FAR, a 61-cubic-inch OHV export road racer—leaves no trace in the historical record.

"Earlenbaugh deserves a lot of credit because he made a good showing with his home-made 45."

A second bike was in the running by June, when Herb Reiber set a new AMA record piloting a 45 OHV twin. In July, it was observed at Dayton that "Herb Reiber, the Lone Star from Wisconsin, (was) riding one of those 'home brew' 45 Harleys." At Muskegon, Earlenbaugh and Moore competed on "homemade 45-inch jobs." Earlenbaugh took second place. Describing his bike, *MotorCycling* said, "The Milwaukee sheik . . . was sporting his own home brew two-port Harley job, a neat outfit and a real display of engineering skill. Herb Reiber also sports a job like Earlenbaugh's."

In August, the *Enthusiast* admitted something new was in the wind when reporting on the New Munster, Wisconsin, hillclimb: "All kinds of shooting irons were on the slant. Some 'Home-Brew' 45's and some that weren't home brew. . . . Art Earlenbaugh,

the Milwaukee sheik, took his 'cellar made' 45 Harley-Davidson over the wall in the 45 event. Which, of course, was considerable show for Art and his 'laboratory model.' "

This is an extremely interesting statement. Was Hap hinting that Earlenbaugh's "cellar made" bike was a 45 OHV that was not Home-Brew? Might not "laboratory model" be code for Harley's own experimental race shop? Was it coincidence that both Harley's experimental and racing departments during these years were indeed located downstairs in a "cellar" at Juneau Avenue?

Whatever their true background, by mid-1928 at least two nearly identical 45-cubic-inch Two-Cam/OHVs were being ridden by Milwaukee men with good factory connections. Apparently Harley-Davidson decided to keep these machines low key, opting not to officially publicize their experimental, quasi-factory status. That wouldn't be unusual for the secretive, sometimes unpredictable Motor Company.

In 1929, the Two-Cam/OHV temporarily fell by the wayside when the hot factory DAH began cleaning up the competition. But Bill Knuth wasn't done with the Two-Cam/OHV yet. After 1930 he used it as a basis for another 45 OHV hillclimber: "Knuth's Special."

What Knuth did (again probably with factory help) was saw off the cam chest on the Two-Cam bottom end and then weld on a four-camshaft cam chest removed from the D model 45-cubic-inch road bike. Ignition was by a rear-mounted magneto, chain driven from a sprocket mounted on the rear exhaust camshaft. The 21 OHV-style Peashooter heads were retained and may have been specially cast.

This four-camshaft layout gave Knuth's Special a straight pushrod angle, overhead-valves, and a racing-strength bottom end for a high-performance 45-cubic-inch motor. These were run in the proven FHAD hillclimb chassis. Chuck Wesholski, who has studied these motors, commented that "the Knuth Specials were *real* special, reflecting insider factory connections and a very intelligent and imaginative mechanical mind."

On a hillclimber all you had was a throttle and kill-button. The 1920s and early 1930s were the heyday of the slant artist.

While the transmission looks stock, hillclimb bikes were single-speed. Lever beneath the exhaust pipe is for putting the bike into gear. Hillclimb engine survival is high because bikes were built tough and runs lasted only 45 seconds or less.

Knuth's Specials were as good as factory hillclimbers. Accounts such as "Knuth's Klimbers are . . . copping all the bacon . . . riding Special 45 Harley-Davidson overhead jobs" were common fare in the motorcycle press. They allowed Bill Knuth to brag, "The[se] motors . . . are the most highly developed internal combustion engines in the world, developing about 1 horsepower per cubic inch and turning over as fast as 125 times per second."

No side-valve or F-head could match that. This gave Milwaukee plenty to chew on, because Harley-Davidson had more tricks up its sleeve.

71

CHAPTER 9
CHANGING TECHNOLOGY

The year 1929 was pivotal for Harley-David-son. Three engine types were built: F-heads, side-valves, and overheads. But this was the last gasp for the F-head, and by 1931 the 21 OHV was gone too. By then, Harley's lineup was entirely devoted to the side-valve engine.

The side-valve seemed destined to rule forever. The Great Depression and a further decline in Motor Company profits seemed to ensure it. Behind the scenes, how-ever, a different scenario was being played out at the Milwaukee factory.

In early 1929, H-D's engineering department graphed the horsepower curves of 15 models—from the 21 Single to the prototype VL. When Harley fans discuss this data, it's inevitably a shouting match over the perfor-mance merits of the JDH versus the VL. But that's like arguing about which dinosaur was baddest. The evolutionary winner was the little 21 OHV.

Although putting out just 12 peak horsepower, the 21 OHV did it with 350 cc, while it took the Big Twins a full 1,000 to 1,200 cc to make their 15 horsepower (Model J), 28 horsepower (prototype Model VL), or 29 horsepower (Model JDH). But *where* the 21 OHV made its power tells the full

> ## "There is no argument but what we should have a faster . . . job."
> —Joe Ryan,
> **H-D Service Manager**

story. While the D-, J-, and V-series bikes reached peak horsepower between 2,800 and 4,000 rpm, the little 21 OHV peaked at 4,800 rpm. After that its power fell off gradually compared to the F-head and side-valve motors, whose breathing ability fell off abruptly.

In fact, at 4,800 rpm, the J model's horse-power had fallen *below* that of the little 21 OHV. Even the horsepower of the new 45-cubic-inch side-valve came per-ilously close to 21 OHV levels at 4,800 rpm. The new C model—a 500 cc side-valve single—was 2 horsepower shy of 21 OHV peak output.

The superior breathing and winding charac-teristics of the overhead-valve engine weren't lost on Harley's engineers. They knew that if the Two-Cam/OHV or DAH hillclimb motors were plotted with those others, they'd blow the top off of the chart.

Always conservative Harley-Davidson, who for years painted their bikes duck boat green, now took a fresh look at the motorcycle market. If the VL was better than the Two-Cam JDH, it wasn't much bet-ter. The VL weighed more (528 pounds vs. 413 pounds by H-D's own specs) and still ran the archaic total-loss oiling system with its mysterious auxiliary handpump.

In spite of Harry Ricardo's work, the side-valve combustion chamber still had major defects. With its angles and corners and twists and turns

By the early 1930s, the side-valve engine carried the entire Harley-Davidson line. This 1933 VLD, owned by Mark Jonas, sports one of the more interesting paint jobs in H-D history.

you couldn't up the compression and still get it to breathe. Plus, the red hot exhaust valve sat next to the cylinder, causing it to locally overheat, warp, and eat pistons.

This letter to "Uncle Frank" (Hap Jameson) in *The Motorcyclist* is typical: "Uncle, my 1934-74 Harley has turned out to be a smelting furnace. She blew up the other day and upon taking off the cylinder heads I find that the front piston . . . looks like somebody got in there with a welding torch."

This wasn't the performance that riders expected from a motor Harley-Davidson advertised as having a "fighting heart." Riders wanted speed *and* reliability. Roads were rapidly improving, and the trend was toward fast solo bikes. Riders back then liked to "spank the saddle," especially after seeing an overhead-valve hillclimber go over the top.

Harley-Davidson was run by intelligent men. True motorcyclists. They saw the attention OHV race bikes received, and experience had shown the performance and reliability advantages of overhead valves. What better marriage between engineering and sales than to build a glamorous new overhead-valve twin?

Perhaps the original team of William S. Harley and Arthur Davidson—the head of engineering and the head of sales—came to the fore. As the Great Depression tightened its noose around Harley-Davidson, the founders shook the dice one last time when they decided to build a *real* sporting motorcycle, something modern and forward looking—and that meant overhead valves.

The groundwork had been laid with the Eight-Valve racers, the 21 OHV, and the 45 OHV hillclimbers. In 1929–1930, H-D built an experimental 30.50-cubic-inch (500 cc) OHV single with a recirculating oil system in road-bike trim. In 1930, they took the 45 OHV DAH hillclimb twin engine and modified it with a recirculating oil system. Then they stuffed it into a road-racing package as the DAR export model. With this bike, Harley-Davidson essentially created the Sportster 27 years ahead of schedule.

It's curious that Bill Harley's engineers didn't use the DAH/DAR engine as the basis for a road-legal overhead-valve twin. Maybe after experience with the 45 and 74 side-valves, they didn't like all those noisy, wear-prone

The VL engine was not totally satisfactory for high-speed work. Piston failure in the big side-valve engine was common, but few riders in the early 1930s imagined that the side-valve's days were numbered.

While a substantial and good-looking machine, the 45 side-valve wasn't much faster than the 21 OHV. This nice 36RLD1072 belongs to Mark Jonas.

angles. There is also great similarity between the shape of the JDH cam gear cover and that found on the Knucklehead, only slightly restyled and flipped around to the front. Even the Knucklehead's "diamond" primary chain cover is a modification of the earlier JD style.

Knowing how Harley did things, the many similar features between the Two-Cam/OHV and the Knucklehead are probably not coincidental. Most likely, Bill Harley and his engineers knew they could do better than the 4-camshaft layout used on the D, VL, and DAH, then cast around for a way out. The Two-Cam/OHV was fresh in mind and looked like a good place to start. Milwaukee was fond of the old F-head motor, especially in Two-Cam form. Its origin went back to 1903.

cam gears. Because when they began work on a "sump oiler" twin in 1931, they started with a blank sheet of paper—or did they?

Maybe not. If the thinking of some modern enthusiasts is correct, the inspiration for the Knucklehead engine may have come from a bike in Milwaukee's then recent past: the 1928 Two-Cam/OHV experimental hillclimber.

As no factory records have yet surfaced, this conclusion is still tentative. Those who worked on these bikes are all dead. But compare the Two-Cam/OHV with the 1936 EL model, and then decide for yourself. Placed side by side these two motors show hauntingly similar features.

Both machines have hemi-head, overhead-valve V-twin engines. Both share the paired detachable lifter blocks inherited from the JDH. Both display the same unique splayed pushrod

This later UL side-valve cut-a-way shows its simple but inefficient valve layout in an air-cooled engine. Exhaust valve location near the piston bore resulted in hot spots and premature piston failure. Motor courtesy Mike Lange.

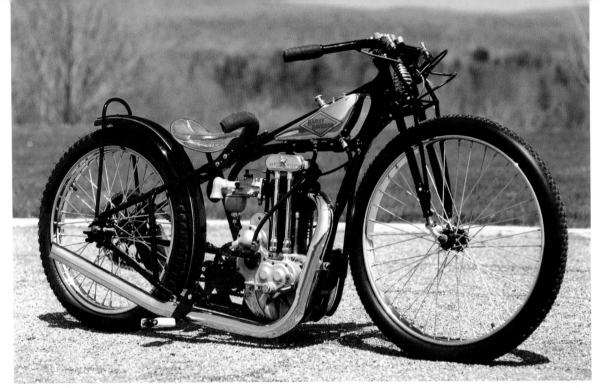

The engine in this 1934 30.50-cubic-inch (500 cc) CAC cinder-track racer was another step in H-D overhead-valve technology. David and Regina Hinze own this hot little racer.

The 1934 CAC has a more Knucklehead-like rocker housing instead of the plates formerly used on the 21 OHV and other Harley overheads. Owner R. L. Jones.

That was *their* motor. What better place to start when working up the Knucklehead?

Traditionally the VL has stood like a brick wall between the JDH Two-Cam and the 1936 EL model in the Big Twin's pedigree. With the Two-Cam/OHV hillclimber in the picture, however, we may have found the logical missing link in the Harley-Davidson line of descent, and thus the lost daddy of everyone's favorite old Harley: the Knucklehead.

Milwaukee may have built a machine even closer to the Knucklehead with the 1929 export FAR model. The FAR is a *real* mystery machine. It only appears on the 1929 list of factory racing bikes. In 1930, it was replaced with the four-camshaft DAR export road racer.

Being an F-series racing bike, the FAR would have used the Two-Cam bottom end. But it also had overhead-valves, as evidenced by the terse factory description: "29FAR 1000cc (61 cu. in.) 3 Speed Racer—Export (Overhead Valves)."

Here perhaps we find the ultimate Knucklehead ancestor. The FAR was 61 cubic inches—same

This experimental Knucklehead-like single is marked "XX W-1." It has a bottom end more closely resembling a side-valve's and appears to have two camshafts. Single oil pump suggests total-loss oil system. Cam cover looks Knucklesque. A real mystery. Motor courtesy Harley-Davidson Archives.

Larger head-finning on the Knuck single suggests stationary engine use. Most other parts differ from production ELs, often significantly. It's unclear how this factory experimental fits into the development of the EL, but it shows the direction Harley was moving by the early 1930s.

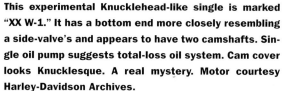

as the EL—and was set up as a road racer with a three-speed transmission. Possibly it ran a recirculating oil system. A sump oiler would make sense on a road racer. The DAR that replaced it had one.

Unfortunately, no further information or photo of the FAR is known to exist. We can only speculate

whether it was a sump oiler and whether its overhead-valve heads, cylinders, and pistons were lifted from the 1929 CA, a 30.50-cubic-inch (500 cc) OHV racing model. With a 4-inch stroke, this configuration would have yielded 60.12 cubic inches (985 cc) in a twin. It isn't difficult to imagine the

In 1936, H-D created a masterpiece with the 61 OHV, here illustrated by Mark Wall's superbly restored 36EL1002. Wall discovered this super-historic motorcycle in Wisconsin and brought it back to its original pristine condition.

boys at H-D trying the FAR prototype around Milwaukee and liking its gutsy potential very much.

If this theory is correct. Harley's talented engineers had little trouble redesigning these Two-Cam/OHV hybrids into a new motor. The prototype EL also included ideas from Bill Harley's own fertile mind. Noteworthy, was an elegant new camshaft arrangement and recirculating oil system. a patent for which was granted in 1938.

This artistic still life of a 1937 EL head, shows the 1936–1937-style "cup" enclosures around the valve springs. Cups and return oil lines to the rear side of rocker housing was a last-minute fix on the 1936 model. Note period tools.

78

Early 1936 parts are clearly visible on 36EL1002. Until the mid-1950s, engine serial numbers began with "1000," thus this motor was the third EL assembled. Only discovery of the original 1903 prototype would surpass this machine's historical value.

Harley designers had gotten plenty of practice over the years, and the perfectly proportioned EL model shows it. Not registered in 1936, 36EL1002 appeared in 1937 with license plate number 52. In 1936, it may have been dealer Erik Eichmann's demonstrator in Sheboygan, Wisconsin.

In 1936, the big 80-cubic-inch VLH side-valve appeared. While a bigger engine, H-D test riders couldn't break 100 miles per hour with it. Scott Ranson owns this handsome example.

The new design was based on a four-lobed, single camshaft. This was a significant adaptation and improvement over the Two-Cam engine. The relocated and larger breather gear in the prototype EL supplied the cam lobes and roller tappets with many times the oil previously thought possible. The overhead-valve rocker arms were also oiled automatically. Just the ticket for a high-revving, high-performance overhead-valve engine. In this manner, Harley's pre-VL line of Big Twins metamorphosed into the immortal Knucklehead.

By using the Two-Cam/OHV as the basis for the 61 OHV, Bill Harley maintained the lineage of his original 1903 motor. Unlike previously thought, there was no break with the past. While new, the Knucklehead wasn't really new at all. And through the same evolutionary process, this continuity has remained true through subsequent motors to the present day.

CHAPTER 10

DREAM BABIES

The 61 OHV model introduced in 1936 was a combination of long experience and modern engineering. Testing Knucklehead prototypes EX-6 and 35EL1002 west of Jefferson, Wisconsin, in the summer of 1935, H-D test riders broke 100 miles per hour. The new 80-cubic-inch VLH side-valve wasn't capable of such speeds.

Later, Harley-Davidson revealed its overhead-valve strategy. "For years our engineers had a vision of a new motorcycle—one that would eliminate . . . the problems inherent with the conventional design of the day . . . that would retain all the best of the past and incorporate all those new principles that would produce a motorcycle unparalleled in performance and efficiency."

In the 61 OHV, riders found their dream come true. The first unveiling came at the Harley-Davidson dealers' convention at Milwaukee in late 1935. Advance billing for this national conference, the first in five years, made the dealers nuts for something new—and they got it.

The late Tom Vandegrift, then dealer in Albert Lea, Minnesota, recalled in a 1997 interview: "It was announced we would have a sensation. They had everybody's vision setting on there. Then they pulled the cover off it. We always expected to see something new, but that 61 was radically different

"This is a 5,000 rpm motor."
—Uncle Frank

because it was an overhead. Afterwards everybody got in there and crowded around so that you couldn't get at it."

Almost every part on the 61 OHV was new. The only things recognizable from the VL were the fenders and generator. The new double-cradle frame divorced the EL from the old loop-frame days forever. The fork went back to the 21 Single's tubular style, beefed up for Big Twin duty. Tires were 4.00x18s, as found on the 45 twin.

The new transmission was the traditional Harley gearbox revamped into an indestructible, constant-mesh four-speed. Built-in instruments formed Bill Harley's patented integral dash. The combined oil tank/battery box was another patented feature. The gas tanks were sleek, teardrop-shaped units—so impressive that H-D still uses them today. The engine can only be described as a masterpiece of performance, reliability, and mechanical beauty.

While the younger dealers marveled at this glittering new apparition of the motorcycle world, the older dealers nodded and smiled, knowing that in the 61 OHV, the king of motorcycles had been reborn.

Reborn because old-timers recalled the famous overheads of their youth—dealers such as Dudley Perkins, who handled the futuristic Jefferson OHV before he became a Harley dealer. Uncrating a new Jefferson twin in 1913, he found it good for 78 miles per hour—not bad when the hot 1928–1929 JDH Two-Cam topped out at 85.

This exquisite 36EL, owned by George and Kathy Pardos, sports the deluxe chrome package. In the minds of many Harley enthusiasts, the styling peak attained in 1936 has never been surpassed.

At the evening banquet. tales of early American overheads filled the room—ghostly names such as Breed. Royal Pioneer. Jefferson. Kenzler-Waverley. P.E.M.. Pope. and the fantastic overhead-valve. overhead-camshaft Cyclone. Behind these nostalgic musings was the joy that in the 61 OHV this superior engine type had come round again.

No test rides were allowed at the November conference. probably because the engineering and

experimental departments were still frantically developing an oil recovery system for the exposed valve stems and springs. Yet. on the basis of a single look. many dealers placed orders for the new EL.

Another superb Mark Wall restoration is 36EL2517. In the optional Maroon-with-Nile green paint scheme, this bike is incredibly flashy and good looking even with very little chrome, and would be the centerpiece of any antique Harley collection.

The styling of the 36EL wasn't slack from any angle. No motorcycle in history had such a long, thoughtful development and subsequent influence. This model links the original Harley-Davidson Motor Co. with today's bikes.

One was Bill Borer, the LaCrosse, Wisconsin, dealer who, mere hours after the November event, was hollering at Art Blixt for an EL. On December 6, Blixt wrote back, "I haven't seen a single 61 shipment as yet on any of the factory daily shipping lists which I receive every day." Borer had to wait for this later note from Joe Kilbert, "We shipped you a 61 overhead on January 17."

This narrows the long-held controversy as to when the first ELs left the Milwaukee factory. Records from Guy Webb's St. Paul dealership show that 36EL1137 and 36EL1144 were shipped on January 24. These dates jibe with the first public notice of a 61 in the *Enthusiast*, telling of a February 2 win at an Oregon endurance run.

As Harley serial numbers started with 1000, this leaves the first 138 61 OHV motors (those below 36EL1137) to account for. It's doubtful that large a number was shipped before January 17. These were probably held back for refitting with the last-minute fix of oil cups and return lines. This cured the original messy arrangement of oil applied directly to bare valve parts exposed to the airstream. Some old-timers recall early 36EL heads being replaced by the factory. Mystery surrounds the first Knucklehead.

Harley-Davidson furthered the ELs mystique by first playing the 61 OHV cautiously and then bragging about it afterwards. In February, the factory warned dealers only to sell the new model to those who would have nothing else. Joe Kilbert counseled them in a letter. "If you have any prospects who will . . . quit [riding] . . . unless they can get a job like the 61, by all means, sell them the 61 o.h.v."

By April, delivery time of 61s had improved to two weeks, although dealers were warned "*not to go out and sell a lot of 61s.*" By July, an unexpected demand for the established models made delivery time for the 61 OHV even better. William H.

continued on page 88

In 1937, the big side-valves were updated with the EL recirculating oil system, and 61 styling. This well-accessorized 1937 UH belongs to Dale Cashman.

Mark Jonas' 37EL1970 shows the oil tank painted to match the bike's gas tanks, which was unique to that year. A nice touch but tough to keep clean. Authentic restorations rely on rich paint and the sheer mechanical beauty of the original design.

Joe Petrali's record breaker, inside H-D Archives. This bike did 136.183 miles per hour at Daytona in 1937. It runs a 1915 fork, JD wheels, and hand-built frame. H-D's Ray Schlee, when cleaning the bike, saved the Daytona Beach sand caught in the frame. The original seat and fender are missing.

The 1939 Knuckleheads had a nice two-tone paint job that Harley has been using again recently. This was the last year of the lean 1930s look for the 61 OHV. The bike is 39EL2305, owned by Mark Jonas.

The only rival to the 61 OHV in Harley's line-up was the 80-cubic-inch ULH side-valve Sport Solo. While massive, the 80 couldn't match the smaller 61 in sustained high-speed durability. Owner of 40ULH4606 is Mark Jonas.

The big side-valve engine was easy starting, distinctive looking, and good for low- to mid-speed work. But by 1941, the overhead twins were outselling the big side-valves.

By 1941, H-D engineering reached another plateau. The 45 engine would change little over the next three decades until its retirement in the 1970s. Mark Jonas owns 41WLD7327.

You have to look twice to see the difference between the 45 and Big Twin side-valves. The two bikes looked similar except that the rear chains came off opposite sides.

continued from page 83

Davidson, who was then in sales, wrote. "Dealers can get 61s . . . on very short notice. . . . (that) gives us a chance to utilize the . . . side valve models . . . for police and commercial sales."

In spite of a few inevitable first year flaws, the 61 OHV performed well. Its quick acceptance by dealers and riders alike, delighted the factory. Confidence rising, Milwaukee crowed with typical 1930s Harley-Davidson bombast: "With years of development behind the new model . . . with 70,000 hours of testing, we knew we were bringing out a new motorcycle that would eclipse everything ever produced before."

What the factory didn't mention, however, was that Lothar A. Doerner, William S. Harley's "right-hand assistant" during the EL's creation, was killed that July testing a new 1937 model near Wisconsin's little Mississippi River town of Victory.

Unlike the 21 OHV, whose quiet introduction in 1926 was followed by a phasing out a few years later, the 61 OHV took hold and never let go. In 1937, the side-valves were redesigned along 61 OHV lines. But while the UL (74 cubic inches) and ULH (80 cubic inches) were nice bikes if not pushed hard, extinction for the big side-valve was on the horizon. As early as February 1936, *Bill Knuth's Tattler* said, "George Feith is getting an 80 in maroon and cream and looking forward to a race with Kelly to decide whether the 61 really has it over the 80. Who will win?"

Harley-Davidson already knew the answer. One factory guy wrote to dealers in 1936, "Here is a model that the motorcycle enthusiast takes right to his heart. It has the class, the lines, the features that make a motorcycle enthusiast want to say— 'How much will you allow me on my hack for one of these dream babies?' "

At the Milwaukee factory this change was soon evident. In 1936, the only Harley *or* Davidson with a 61 OHV registered for street use was William J. Harley (Bill Harley's older son), who

This style dash went back to 1939. The classic Harley layout that originated with the 36EL is evident on Jonas' 41WLD. Tank-mounted speedo and ignition switch grace Harley models today, as well as new copycat bikes.

Only a few 1942 civilian models were built. This 74 OHV, photographed at Davenport, is one of about 800 FLs built that year. Big tires and metal tank badges took away from earlier sleek looks of 1930s EL models.

had 36EL1517. By late 1940, however, Walter C. Davidson was riding 40EL1420; William J. Harley, 40EL3157; William H. Davidson, 40E3185; and John Harley, 41FL3900. Only Gordon Davidson stuck to the flathead—40U2196.

Numbers tell the tale. In 1936, H-D built "nearly 2,000" 61 OHVs. (Factory sources state 1,704 while serial number analysis suggests nearer 1,950.) That same year 5,480 big sidevalves left the factory. By 1941, 5,149 EL and FL overheads were built compared to 4,145 big sidevalves. That year just 420 80-cubic-inch Special

Sport Solo ULH models were built—the OHV twins' only real competition.

With the coming of the 74 OHV in 1941, the big flathead was doomed. Ironically, it also killed the 61 OHV. Connie Schlemmer, who worked at Otto Ramer's Omaha dealership in the 1930s, recalled. "We had one fellow [Fave] who would order a new 61 every year. . . . In 1940 he . . . was talking with Hap Jameson [who] offered to take [Fave's] buddy seat passenger in his sidecar, which was hooked to a prototype 74 OHV engine, and Fave said he could hardly keep up with the sidecar with his 61."

93

Still riding. Bruce Linsday with his 1937 Knucklehead. He took a 38EL to Germany, then rode it to Russia and back. These bikes run!

After the EL was introduced in 1941, sales of the EL dropped off drastically. In 1952 (their last year), only 960 61 OHV Panheads were built compared to 5,740 74 OHVs.

Some thought the EL was smoother and went fast enough. One modern rider who agrees is Bruce Linsday. Probably the most dedicated Knucklehead fan alive. Linsday rides his original

Close-up of a 74-cubic-inch OHV engine shows the mighty Knucklehead at its peak. No other design has shown such staying power; indeed, Harley motors today are still based on the Knucklehead.

1937 and 1938 ELs like most guys *don't* ride their new bikes. He's crossed the country at least 15 times on Knuckleheads. If that wasn't enough, he and his girlfriend once took his 1938 EL to Germany and rode to Moscow and back.

"I think it's the best thing Harley *ever* did," Linsday said. "The 61 was a better combination than the 74. The 61 had the small diameter flywheels and the 18-inch [road] wheels. The bigger [16-inch] tire made them handle like a tank. It was no improvement. Those 61 Knuckleheads are smooth and well balanced. They're an amazingly good engine. . . . I'm still impressed by them."

CONCLUSION

THE GHOST IN THE MACHINE

In the 36EL and 41FL models lays the combined genius of those thousands of Harley-Davidson workers who reached the peak of their talents in the 1920s and 1930s. With the Knucklehead, the founders immortalized in iron their concept of the ideal motorcycle.

Yet the 61 and 74 OHV models could trace their origin directly back to the 1903 prototype, which over the decades had been updated and improved, and in 1928 was converted to full overhead-valve in the experimental Two-Cam/OHV hillclimber. This bike in turn inspired the 1936 and 1941 Knuckleheads—the first real overhaul of the Harley-Davidson motorcycle since 1903.

> **"It is hard to tell if we adore these old bikes because they have a soul or because they assist us with ours."**
>
> —**Martin Jack Rosenblum**

The Knucklehead came none too soon: by 1950, the four founders of Harley-Davidson were dead. By then much had changed. Another world war had come and gone. The competition had a new face. Riders and bikes were changing too. America was entering the modern era.

Yet the founders' final and greatest creation lived on. For the Knucklehead embodied more than just good looks and sustainable high speed. It was the first Harley-Davidson with timeless appeal. Call it what you want—heritage, prestige, mystique, nostalgia, work-of-art, soul, spirit, daemon, orenda, kami, or dream baby—it's all the same. It's the truth behind the slogan "More than a machine," or more poetically perhaps: *the ghost in the machine.*

It's what drives some to adorn their bodies with Harley-Davidson symbols. Why Japanese enthusiasts—countrymen of the builders of the

This 1915 twin shows original inlet-over-exhaust valve (F-head) layout used on all pre-1930 Big Twins. With a few changes you'd have the original 1903 motor. Engine courtesy Mike Lange.

Electra-Glide. Plus the choppers. the factory customs. the Springers. the Fat Boys. and the Bad Boys. Then toss in the dizzying array of Japanese. American. and European copycat bikes. No matter what name. insignia. or slogan they hide behind. the Knucklehead inspired them all.

The current Motor Company knows it. They know they must retain the mystique of Bill Harley's 1936 creation while competing against world's most advanced double overhead-camshaft. many-cylinder. multi-valve. liquid cooled. computerized. fuel-injected. shaft-drive motorcycles—unexpectedly reject their own techno wonders for an admittedly antiquated Harley-Davidson. essentially the same machine that Bill Harley breathed life into in 1936. Why? As one Japanese rider put it. "My Harley-Davidson is alive."

The Knucklehead is the greatest motorcycle of them all. One has only to look at the present generation of Harley-Davidson Big Twins to see that. The 36EL sired the Panhead. the Shovelhead. the Evolution. and the new Twin Cam 88 motor. It begat the Hydra-Glide. the Duo-Glide. and the

Experimental 45-cubic-inch Two-Cam/OHV hillclimber engine mated Peashooter heads to the Two-Cam bottom end. Cylinders were specially cast. This 1928 Two-Cam bottom is the "direct-action" type with detachable tappet blocks and no cam followers. Bike courtesy Motorcycle Heritage Museum.

This 1936 EL engine (in George and Kathy Pardos' machine) shows hauntingly similar features to the Two-Cam/OHV, although refined and modernized. Decide for yourself whether the Two-Cam/OHV is the missing link in the Big Twin line.

the increasingly sophisticated competition in the 21st century. They realize the stakes. As H-D's head engineer, Earl Werner, said recently, "Trying to innovate while preserving the purity in the heritage. It weighs heavily on all of us."

Harley-Davidson grabbed both future and past with its new 1999 model Twin Cam 88 engine. At first glance the new dual-camshaft layout seems a taboo break with tradition, but clearly, when one

studies Harley's past, it is not. We only have to go back to the progenitor of the Knucklehead—the 1928 experimental Two-Cam/OHV hillclimber—to find what Harley engineers reinvented today.

Coincidence? Maybe. Or maybe the ghost is real after all. Maybe Bill Harley and the Davidson brothers still haunt the bricks and mortar of Juneau Avenue. Maybe, in whispered dreams, they're still calling the shots.

HARLEY-DAVIDSON
CUSTOMS

Tim Remus

Acknowledgments

This book contains more than thirty bikes, which means there are far too many to thank each owner or builder by name. There are, just the same, a few individuals who need to be singled out. Steve Laugtug, for example, must be thanked for allowing me access to his elaborate photo studio. And my lovely and talented wife Mary must be thanked for rinsing all that film in the Motel room sink after the Pepsi can exploded in the cooler. Yes, the same cooler that contained all the film I shot in Daytona.

To all the rest, I have to offer a collective thanks—for showing up on time, for moving the bikes a million times, for filling out the technical sheets, and mostly for being patient.

Russ Tom created a unique ride by combining a FXR chassis with a FLH front end, complete with the big front fender and headlight nacelle.

Introduction

The Harley-Davidson world, and custom Harley-Davidsons in particular, is moving pretty fast these days. What were cutting edge bikes only four or five years ago are now quite common. Every time I go to Sturgis the bikes aren't just better, they're a lot better than they were one year before. The design, the execution, the paint and assembly—all the things required to build a great bike have improved dramatically in the past few years.

There are new people coming into the sport (the ones that some old timers grouse about), and they bring with them new ideas and sophisticated fabrication skills. More riders and enthusiasts means that there's a larger pool of talent and money to draw on. Money attracts parts manufacturers, so there are more parts in the catalogs than ever before. And those parts aren't just widgets or skull-shaped valve caps for your tires. There are some pretty slick new calipers and wheels carved from large chunks, or billets, of aluminum on computerized lathes and mills. Arlen and Cory Ness have introduced a whole line of billet parts, everything from handlebar grips to lifter blocks. And a host of formerly automotive-only companies are hot on their heels with new designs.

New sheet metal designs are turning up, too. Now there are more than two gas tanks in the catalog, presumably because the market is big enough to warrant the tooling required to knock out new shapes. And covering all that sheet metal on the newest bikes is some outrageous paint. The colors offered by House of Kolor and PPG, among others, are nothing short of electric. The new urethane paints are super vibrant, very durable and easier to spray (though they still require caution in their use due to the toxicity of the chemicals). The new paints and increasing skills of the custom painters mean that the new bikes carry brighter reds and softer pearls than ever before.

The Harley-Davidsons in this book represent some of the best of the new breed of customs. Broken down by model "family," I've tried to include both the high-dollar bikes that garner all the press, as well as the less expensive machines built by individuals in home shops. Though the book doesn't detail all the features on the bikes, the captions are as informative as I could make them in order to answer the many questions you'll surely have about each motorcycle.

My own bias runs toward designs that are simple (though there's at least one very gaudy Harley-Davidson included here). I prefer bikes that rely on the strength of the design, rather than the number of widgets or murals, for their good looks. I also feel that custom bikes should be functional with good handling and brakes. The bikes presented here, though varied, reflect my opinions and tend toward the simple and sanitary.

These are good-looking bikes. As much as possible, they represent a cross-section of the custom bikes from Main Street America. I hope to have captured not only the bikes but a little of the energy that the bikes represent. If the book had a soundtrack, it would be the rumble of multiple V-twins running hard down the main drag of Sturgis or Daytona. Can you hear it? Good. Now crank the volume, and open the book.

1 Sportsters

Not Necessarily Basic

A good design has a certain staying power, witness the old VW "bug," the Chevy small-block V-8, and, of course, the Harley-Davidson Sportster. First introduced in 1957 (though the K models were available earlier without the Sportster moniker), the Sportster was and is a great-looking bike. There's nothing extra here, just an engine, a gas tank, and two wheels. As delivered, these are basic motorcycles, well built and well proportioned. Rare is the Sportster that remains basic for very long, however.

In days of yore, the Sportster was the bike to have. The over-forty crowd will remember the magic letters "XLCH." They held a certain allure for any kid with a little gasoline in

Simple and tasty, Jim and Jeannie Shaller's Sportster started life as a stock, 1993, 883. With the addition of a few body pieces, a nice paint job, and some accessories, this "little Harley" is transformed into a striking motorcycle. Grips and mirrors are from the Kuryakyn catalog as is the air cleaner, which gives the Sportster the look of a larger bike with a killer motor.

The unique gas tank is a factory CR item. This is actually the second tank. The first was mounted solid to the bike and developed cracks due to vibration. Underneath all the shine is a 74-cubic-inch Ironhead engine with a stroker bottom end, ported heads, S&S carburetor, and fabricated exhaust based on a set of XLCR pipes.

his veins because the hot rod Sportster was said to be the fastest bike on the street. When the chopper phenomena hit in the late 1960s, Sportsters remained tremendously popular. Bike shows of the period were filled with Sportsters modified with hardtail kits and long, springer front forks.

Eventually the Big Twin replaced the Sportster as the bike to have. Hot rodders say it's hard to beat cubic inches, and the Big Twin offered more cubes and more potential for raw horsepower. Big Twins became more "macho" than Sportsters and more likely to be modified and customized. Sportsters became the bike to ride rather than the bike to customize.

But there have always been die-hard Sportster supporters among the ranks of Harley-Davidson owners—men and women who will ride nothing else, and who sell one Sportster just to buy another. In the past, anyone who wanted to customize a Sportster had to rely on hand-fabricated or adapted parts, as the number of aftermarket parts designed for the Sportster was relatively small.

That situation has changed recently, and the major aftermarket companies like Custom Chrome, Drag Specialties, and Nempco all offer tanks, fenders, wheels, and a variety of accessories built strictly for the Sportster line. You can make a Sportster look like a Big Twin or a cafe racer with parts right out of the catalog. Or you can mix and match and create your own version of the ideal Sportster.

Bob Heinze used a 1977 Sportster as a starting point for creating a personalized Sportster CR. By combining a factory CR gas tank with a cafe style fairing and minimal rear fender, Bob created a unique Sportster with the look of a CR. While the factory CR used black on black for a sinister look, Bob's cafe racer uses red flames over burgundy base paint, combined with plenty of chrome and polish for a very bright package.

Left, this bike is a combination of off-the-shelf parts and hand-fabricated hardware. The front fairing and fender are from Arlen Ness, and the gas tank is from Harley-Davidson. Unique oil tank, fender struts, and exhaust were built by Donnie Smith. Cast wheels are from Harley-Davidson and painted to match the bike.

Bill Messenbrink's Sportster is based on a 1977 frame stretched two inches to accept an XLCR gas tank. The cafe fairing, longer tank, scalloped paint job, and sleek profile make the bike look trim and fast. The Sportster taillight is molded into what was an FL front fender and mounted to the bike with modified FX fender struts. Under the fender sits a 150x16-inch tire, which requires off-set sprockets so the chain will clear the tire.

In the past couple of years, buying a new Harley meant knowing your dealer, paying a premium, or waiting patiently for your name to come up on a long list. The most popular of the hyper-popular Harleys are the Big Twin models. This means that recent buyers often get a Sportster simply because they can have one today instead of waiting until three years from next Tuesday. These new buyers then take advantage of the parts in the catalogs to create a bike of their own.

Savvy buyers understand that the Sportster to have is the smaller 883 model. It's a lot cheaper than the 1200, and it can be bumped to the larger capacity with relative ease. With the additional displacement and a few key parts, a 1200 Sportster will put out more than seventy horsepower at the rear wheel—enough to turn the "little Harley-Davidson" into a true hot rod that will stomp most of its bigger brothers.

The bikes shown here represent both ends of the spectrum. The Ironheads are built with stretched frames and plenty of hand-fabricated parts while the other bike is a more modern Evolution model built

The front spoiler doubles as a small oil tank and was fabricated by Messenbrink. Not only does it add capacity to the system, it also acts as a radiator to keep the engine cool. An Arlen Ness cafe fairing helps give the bike its go-fast look. Lower fork legs are chrome plated as are the Harley-Davidson calipers. The unusual front fender is a Sportster unit turned end-for-end and modified with extra skirting.

Left, Bill Messenbrink's old
Ironhead engine uses an S&S bottom end and 0.030-over pistons for a displacement of 74 cubic inches. An older S&S Series-B carb feeds gas and air to ported heads with valves operated by four Sifton minus-minus camshafts. Each cylinder head is tapped for an extra spark plug, which are fired by Dyna coils and a Dyna single-fire ignition. Chrome-plated fins on the heads and cylinders shine brightly.

with aftermarket parts. Like all good cus-tomized motorcycles, paint plays a key part in all four designs. The bikes looks are very different from one another and help to illustrate the point that a good builder need not be limited by the basic nature of a Sportster. Though they start out kind of short and basic, they certainly don't have to stay that way.

At nearly forty years of age, the Sport-ster shows no gray hairs and seems, in fact, to be the eternal adolescent. Never overweight and never out of style, the Sportster remains a wonderful motorcycle and a good starting point for a personal-ized Harley-Davidson.

Left, all that glitters is not chrome. In this case the glitter comes from powder-coated rocker boxes, engine cases, and exhaust pipes combined with a flat black Dell'Orto carburetor and cylinders.

Above, Orville built himself a very tasty Ironhead Sportster with some unusual wheels, a solo seat, cafe fairing, and a nice black with gold leaf paint job.

2 The FXR Models

Born to Boogie

Originally known as Super Glide II, the FXR series Harley-Davidsons were introduced late in 1981. Though the lines at first seem similar to those of the earlier FX Super Glide, the FXR was a whole new motorcycle.

The frame, for example, was computer designed to be five times stiffer than the old FX frame. Instead of bolting the engine directly into the frame, it was (and still is) supported by a three-point suspension system (known on the street as "rubber mounted"). Instead of a four-speed, the new bike came with a five-speed trans-

The nice orange paint job by Jerry Scherer, the extra fork rake, and lowered stance give Donnie Smith's FXR a nice, clean look. Note the molded frame, paneled area under the seat, and use of paint instead of chrome for many of the parts and accessories. Ported heads—shaved for more compression—work in conjunction with the Andrews EV3 cam, Series-E carburetor, and Arlen Ness/SuperTrapp exhaust pipe to produce good, usable horsepower for the street.

Like the frame, the sheet metal on this bike consists of modified Harley-Davidson components. The taillight is molded into the FXR fender, and the gas tank is missing the console, instead using a small "Donnie Smith special" gas cap. Brake calipers are from GMA, and the wheels are polished and painted Harley-Davidson items.

mission. Though the first bikes were equipped with the Shovelhead engine, by 1984 all FXR Harley-Davidsons were equipped with the Evolution engine.

The engineers designed the new frame with the battery and oil tank tucked neatly under the seat. Thus these bikes seem much more streamlined than the older bikes. The wheelbase on the FXR, at 64.7 inches is just more than 2 inches longer than the 62.3 inch wheelbase of the early Super Glides. The combination of a longer frame and tucked in oil tank and battery give the FXR a smoother look than the older FX.

Well-known bike builder Dave Perewitz has commented that when you strip an FXR they get long and low—and that seems to be the way most customized FXRs turn out. Though you can build an FXR into any kind of bike you want, the long, lean look seems to prevail. When Arlen Ness bolted a small cafe fairing to the front of a slammed FXR he started another styling trend that continues to this day. To say the catalogs are filled with parts for the FXR is an understatement. A mountain of aftermarket fenders, side covers (from Arlen again), seats, and exhausts prove that this is a very popular bike in customizing circles.

With the rubber-mounted engine, a stiff frame, and good suspension, the FXR is a bike that lends itself to a certain hot rod theme. An FXR can be hopped up, customized, and even lowered (as long as the owner doesn't go too far) and remain a ridable, comfortable bike that handles well. With an FXR, a prudent customizer

Wayne wanted a radical but ridable bike. Jim Thompson of Cylinder Head Service installed all new bottom end components but retained the stock stroke. The heads were reworked with a good port job, new, larger valves, and higher-quality springs and keepers. Wayne did the final assembly himself, using a Redshift 575 cam, chrome moly pushrods, and an S&S "shorty" carburetor.

Wayne Benson's FXR benefits from a much-modified frame—the rear section has been widened and the front section is brand new. Note that the flattened fender rails are part of the frame. With all that custom frame work, stock sheet metal just wouldn't cut it. The gas tank started life as a police tank, then was stretched ten inches at the back and shaped to wrap around the front of the Danny Gray seat. To fill the new, wider rear frame section, the stock FXR fender was widened nearly two inches. In front, an aftermarket fender was grafted to a FXR fender bracket. When all the fabrication was finished, the frame and all the sheet metal were molded and finished by Don Perewitz of Cycle Fab fame.

can have his cake and eat it too by building a good-looking bike with all the right stuff—one that can still be ridden on a daily basis. In fact, one of the bikes seen here—the orange FXR— is the daily rider for well-known customizer Donnie Smith.

Though the bike remains very popular, the FXR models have been phased out by Harley-Davidson to be replaced by the new Dyna Glide line. Men and women on the street don't seem to care that the model is on its way out. They're still building FXR bikes with everything from modified stock V-twins to full-on stroker motors with nitrous oxide. Forks are kicked out with extra rake to create what Donnie Smith calls, "A bike with an attitude." With shorter fork tubes or spring kits for the front forks and shorter rear shocks, the height comes down (more easily than

Tom from Carlton Harley-Davidson in Mantua, Ohio, massaged Andy's Evo with ported heads, an Andrews EV3 camshaft, and a Series E S&S carburetor. A good motor should show as well as go, so Andy used chrome rocker covers, primary cover, coil cover, an S&S air cleaner to contrast with the otherwise Lumina-red V-twin.

Andy Drobnjakovic's FXR features Harley-Davidson forks lowered with a set of White Bros. fork springs. The solid front wheel is from Rev Tech and measures 21 inches in diameter. The front fender and cafe-style fairing are both from the Arlen Ness catalog.

with a Softail by the way), and then it's a matter of choosing the right sheet metal and a sufficiently brilliant paint job.

If there's a trend of late, it's toward longer bikes with custom sheet metal and beautiful, bright paint. The FXR again lends itself to the long look. Some builders can't get enough of a good thing and build FXRs with stretched frames and stretched gas tanks to match. Arlen Ness has capitalized on this concept with his Luxury Liners, which seem to me more like a Dresser than a hot rod FXR (see the Dresser chapter for one example of a very long, low FXR).

The bikes shown in this chapter run the gamut from relatively simple machines to elaborate projects that took many months and many dollars to complete. Some have been lowered, painted, and souped up. Others ride on modified frames with extra rake, equipped with hand-crafted sheet metal and completely polished and chrome-plated engines. Wayne's red FXR is one such bike, built

Drobnjakovic calls this FXR his first "serious" Harley-Davidson. The molded frame and mostly stock sheet metal wear red paint in a Chevy Lumina shade. Some not-so-stock sheet metal is seen at the rear, where the cat's eye taillight is frenched neatly into the rear fender.

Next page upper left, Dan figures he's got 3,500 hours invested in the fabrication of flames, not including final polishing and plating. Dan cut each flame from sheet steel, heated it with a torch to shape it, and then sanded the edges.

Next page lower left, the outside of Dan's V-twin has been treated to two-tone powder coating and engraved and chrome plated covers. Inside there are Wiseco pistons, ported heads, a Crane cam, and a Series-E carburetor from S&S.

121

Drag bars with speedo and tach mounted beneath and a Softail-style rear fender give Ray Puglisi's FXR a sleek look all its own. The paint is white pearl from House of Kolor with hot pink and purple graphics. Note the carb hanging off the wrong side.

Previous page right, Dan Sudnick's FXR features flames in the paint and flames in 3-D. The front fender is from an FLH, narrowed to fit the FXR narrow-glide fork. The rear fender is from an FXR and modified to resemble the front. Juan Villicana from The Fantasy Studio sprayed the wild paint job which took five weeks to complete.

Next page left, Puglisi's FXR uses Rev Tech Wheels and GMA brake hardware mounted to a stock frame. The front fender is from the Arlen Ness catalog; the front and rear of the bike have been lowered two inches.

Next page right, Ray's chrome plated V-twin retains the stock 80-cubic-inch displacement, but that's about all. High compression pistons, ported heads, Crane cam, and a unique intake with two Dell'Orto carbs make this V-twin look and run like nothing else.

Charlie's FXR dates to 1982 and thus uses the Shovelhead for power. This example uses a Sifton #102 camshaft and a S&S Series-E carburetor to improve breathing and performance.

around an FXR frame with a new front frame section, a modified rear section, some very classy sheet metal, and first-class wheels and hardware.

Big, hot rod engines call for fat rear tires, which don't fit easily between the arms of a stock swingarm. This then requires a conversion from the factory belt, to chain drive. That's all fine and good as long as the drive sprocket lines up with the driven sprocket—and the fender is wide enough to cover the new tire. One seemingly small change often begets another and another until very little of the original bike remains.

Variety is the spice of life, as shown by the FXRs in this chapter. Some were built by professionals, and others were bolted together by "amateurs" using all their skill (and probably all their money). No matter, they're all lovely and they're all functional. In the best FXR tradition, these are all hot rod Harleys, and they're all "riders."

3 *Softails*

Never Stock for Long

Designed to look like a true "hardtail," the Harley-Davidson Softail uses a triangulated swingarm and hides the spring/shock units under the transmission. Considered by many to be Harley-Davidson's single best marketing move in the past ten years, the introduction of the Softail gave Harley-Davidson sales a jump-start and created a lot of work for customizing shops as well. Introduced as an extension of the then-current Wide Glide, the addition of Fat Bob tanks, a long Wide Glide fork, and a variety of accessories made the Softail a factory-built custom.

Al Verduzco's Fat Boy wears a great pearl paint job and just enough accessories to set it apart from the crowd. Al's mostly stock Evo breathes through a Kuryakyn air cleaner and expels spent gases through a two-into-one exhaust. A variety of small things help set off this Fat Boy from the crowd, like the drag bars with billet grips, the nice forward controls, and the chrome cover for the rear frame section.

The unusual paint job on the Fat Bob tanks was created by first painting the bike black, then taping off the scallops and spraying them with a splatter gun. The custom dash is an item from the Arlen Ness catalog.

Left, note the extensive use of paint even on things like the headlight housing—a part that would normally be chromed or polished.

Above, Tank Ewsichek's bright Softail rolls on Performance Machine wheels—a 16-inch front and an 18-inch rear. The front fender is from a Heritage, and the rear fender—supported by Custom Chrome fender rails—was created by joining two Heritage fenders.

Bob Lowe's softail is truly an original, made up mostly of hand-formed panels and parts. Wheels are aluminum hoops from Custom Chrome, brake calipers are from The Motor Company.

The V-twin carries high-compression pistons and a Crane cam. Gas and air are mixed in the S&S carb, fired by a Dyna single-fire ignition, and exit via the custom two-into-one exhaust.

Ron Englert formed the unique gas tank from scratch, working sheet steel on an English wheel. FLH-style headlight nacelle has been blended with the bars and the tachometer housing to form a very slick assembly. Note the flush-mount gas cap.

Though it may not look it, this nifty swingarm started life at The Motor Company. Eccentric axle adjusters are the handiwork of Roger Bergei of A.C. Customs. Fabricated taillight housings double as fender struts and look as though they might have come from a 1953 Buick.

Though all Harleys seem destined for modification and customizing by their owners, the Softail seems like the ideal bike for men and women who want to build a motorcycle unlike any other parked at the curb. With an engine solidly bolted into the frame and limited suspension movement, the Softail might not be the road bike an FXR is, but when a bike looks this good who cares about suspension travel?

At the time of its introduction there were only two Softail models. Today the Softail frame is the basis for a at least four separate families of motorcycles. The pop-

Ed Kerr's softail is unlike any other. The more you look, the more you see. The oil tank has "tails" welded on so it better fills the area below the seat. Nifty air cleaner is the work of Ken Rasp and was fabricated from sheet aluminum. The rear of the Softail frame has been cleaned up and modified to neatly accept the fabricated rear fender struts. Between the fender struts is a modified Arlen Ness Taildragger fender with a flush-mount taillight.

The Arlen Ness front fender wraps around a 21-inch spoked rim supported by a Springer fork assembly. Performance Machine four-piston calipers slow it all down.

Left, the floorboards are hand crafted—including the rubber strips—as were the small panels between the primary cover and the frame. The good-looking V-twin features polished cases and cylinders with polished fins (in fact, the lower fins were polished right off the cylinders) all painted red to match the bike.

Wild paint and first class components make for a modern, sophisticated Softail. Mike Ethier's bike uses a stock frame, aftermarket fenders, and modified 5-gallon Fat Bob Tanks. Note the flush-mount taillight and frenched license plate. A low stance was achieved by using White Bros. springs in the front fork and a modified swingarm with Fournales shocks in back.

Left, though the engine displaces only 80 cubic inches, it cranks out 80 horsepower at the rear wheel as measured by the Custom Chrome dynamometer. Power is achieved through the use of modified heads, high lift camshaft, S&S Super G carb, Bartels pipes, and Dyna 2000 single-fire ignition.

Above, derby and inspection covers, as well as the mirrors, are part of the Mirage accessories set from Custom Chrome. Transmission is a stock five-speed with belt-drive to the rear wheel. Billet wheels as well as four-piston brake calipers are from Performance Machine.

ularity of the machine, and the tendency of Softail owners to personalize their bikes, means that the catalogs from the major aftermarket companies are filled with Softail accessories.

Softails lend themselves to a variety of styling themes. The rigid-look frame means they're a natural for any kind of old-time or nostalgic theme. Mix an early-style oil filter, horn, and tool box with the

Everybody wants their bikes long and low. Brad Cullen's yellow Softail was lengthened by mating an Arlen Ness front section to a Harley-Davidson Softail rear frame section. Additional fork rake and low stance enhance the effect of

the stretched frame. To fit the longer frame, the Fat Bob tanks have been lengthened 3-1/2 inches and wrap neatly around the seat. Instead of a conventional dash and gauges, Brad chose a neat "no gauges" dash for the clean look.

Left side shows more of what makes the nostalgia theme work: chrome sprocket cover, tombstone taillight, white grips—to match the white leather seat and pillion—and fringed, white leather lever covers.

right paint job, and the bike suddenly appears much older. Or add a genuinely old fork assembly, as one of our owners did, and the bike looks as though it was built before the war.

If FXR models lend themselves to the long, lean look, Softails lend themselves to the fat profile. Equipped with fat, tail-dragger fenders, Fat Bob tanks, and six-teen-inch wheels on both ends, the bikes are anything but skinny. Maybe this trend is fueled by the aging motorcycle riding population. It seems that as the average age of the riders goes up (and often the weight as well), so does the size and weight of their motorcycles.

Because the shock/spring units are hidden, the bikes take on a completely different look than a FXR or Dyna Glide. Though these bikes are a natural for a chopper look, the lack of visible rear suspension components also make them candidates for

Right, sunfire yellow and linen cream white paint, a chrome tool box, fishtail pipes, and early-style horn all reinforce the old-time theme.

The engine on Mike's ride is nearly stock. The air cleaner is from Drag Specialties. Note the horn, tank logo, oil filter, and the louvered dash panel between the tanks.

Left, Don Hotop doesn't believe in using a lot of off-the-shelf accessories. Thus we see a one-off air cleaner with an interesting milled pattern—a pattern repeated on the ignition and transmission covers and the plug for the oil tank.

Above, there isn't much here that isn't essential to the operation of the motorcycle. The frame is molded with integral fender rails, and the gas tank features a small, custom dash with speedometer. The air dam is a Hotop trademark. Wheels are from Harley-Davidson, polished and painted for extra allure. GMA provided the brake calipers, though the milled pattern is Hotop's own.

an ultra-modern, sophisticated look. Without any shock absorbers in the way, a builder or designer can pay more attention to the sheet metal at the bike's rear. To see just how far you can go with the design of a very slick motorcycle, just check out Bob Lowe's black Softail in this chapter.

Though some riders and builders prefer FXRs and some like a Dresser, there are probably more customized Softails than any other single model. The bikes in this chapter include the already mentioned future-bike look, along with more traditional custom bikes. There are also Fat Boys (but no Fat Girls) with tremendous visual impact, though in truth they remain

If you look closely, you'll see a small 4-Valve logo on the rocker covers that identify this as a V-twin with Fueling Stage III four-valve head kit. The kit includes the four-valve heads two S&S carburetors, and Fueling exhaust.

close to stock. And then there are Softails that retain very little of their original frame or sheet metal. In between are a number of what can only be called, "Main Street Customs," or bikes you might admire as they sit outside a local bar or restaurant.

Ron Rupp's sleek Springer gets its attitude from the extra fork rake and the lower-than-stock height. Ron used visual tricks to lower the bike further, including a lowered front fender and headlight and a lowered rear fender mounted with Arlen Ness fender rails.

Left, the flamed paint job wasn't enough; note the flamed Corbin seat and flamed Arlen Ness billet grips. The 21-inch spoked front rim is combined with an 18-inch Performance Machine rear rim and a 140-series Metzeler tire.

These machines are definitely different from the FXR bikes, and they're different from each other. Some are fat, and some are relatively thin. Some carry the sixteen-inch front wheel close to the frame while others kick a twenty-one-inch spoked rim

way out in front. Most use all of the Harley-Davidson frame, though at least one uses an aftermarket frame. One bike uses a "Softail" frame fabricated from 4130 Chrome Moly steel in conjunction with a swingarm that includes an integral brake caliper cut from two pieces of billet aluminum. Perhaps better suited to the Customs chapter, this particular bike uses modified upside-down forks and sheet

149

The primary drive consists of a special drive pulley with a spring-loaded compensator, a Gates Poly-Chain belt, and a fabricated clutch basket. Little John's idea was to eliminate anything that wasn't essential and to shrink the parts that were. Note the "forward controls" coming off the carved-from-billet primary cover.

Previous page, a "Softail" in design only, Gary Newton's bike was fabricated by Little John Buttera. The frame is 4130 Chrome Moly, and the swingarm—with integral brake caliper—was carved from aluminum billet. The fork is a White Power upside-down unit. Steve Davis crafted the tank, fenders, and oil tank from sheet steel or aluminum.

Right, the gas tank is made up of smaller sheets of aluminum shaped on a power hammer and then welded together. Air is drawn through a hand-hammered air cleaner, mixed with gas by an S&S Super-G carburetor, then fed to ported Harley-Davidson heads. Even the exhaust system was carefully formed by hand to have just the right shape.

Springer fork and early fender create much
of the old look for this modern bike. Both
Wheels are 16-inch Harley-Davidson items
with rechromed rims and stainless spokes.
Note the light bar, Deluxe logo, and nifty front
fender light.

Right, Alan Webber's Hardtail isn't really a
Hardtail, though it isn't really a Softail either.
The hybrid design uses a Softail-type frame
from Tripoli Inc. and a 1946 springer fork
assembly, complemented by sheet metal and
accessories possessing that old-time look.

Next page left, Evo engine gives it away—this
ain't really an old Hardtail. Engine is stock
except for S&S shorty carb and an early-style air
cleaner. Transmission is equipped with Andrews
components for a lower first gear and the
mandatory kick start lever. Cat-eye dash and
Fat Bob tanks look right at home.

Denis' Plante's softail custom bike uses 16-inch rubber on both front and rear. Drag-style handlebars are from a Canadian company called Slight Mod and wear Arlen Ness grips and mirrors. A stock Harley-Davidson rear wheel was modified to fit the front, then chrome plated. The fork is longer than stock and features polished and machined lower legs.

Previous page right, Denis' V-twin retains it's 80-cubic-inch displacement, though it breathes through ported heads with the help of an S&S cam and carburetor and a pair of Bartels' Performance pipes. The unusual white-blue-flamed paint job was designed and applied by the owner.

Plante's Softail Custom turned into a true custom Softail with the addition of a great paint job, a longer front end, new fenders, Corbin seat, and Arlen Ness taillight.

metal fabricated by one of California's most talented "tin men."

These bikes offer a window into the collective imagination of America's gearheads and motorcycle enthusiasts. Before you decry the lack of skill or imagination shown by today's workers, look again at these motorcycles. The old-world skills, the imagination, the willingness to take risks, those seemingly lost abilities are alive and well—in the world of customized Harley-Davidsons.

4 Dressers

Traveling in Style

The first Dresser was born—rather than created—when some rider mounted leather bags and a canvas windshield on some very early model Harley-Davidson. Always close to their riders, the factory first sold these items as part of their own line of accessories and eventually offered the bikes equipped with bags and windshield, or "already dressed" if you will. Personalizing those early bikes was usually done by adding more of the same—more lights, crash guards, and bumpers for the fenders.

Always a solid part of the Harley-Davidson landscape, Dressers were, until recently, seen as "adult" motorcycles.

Left side of Tank's dresser shows it to be the most modern of rides. Note the monochromatic paint job, frenched taillight, coral paint job, and extended fenders. Rear view shows off the cat's eye taillight set into the fender and the total lack of chrome. The bike has been lowered 2 inches at both ends, and extended fenders make it seem lower than it really is.

161

Lenny and Connie Schwartz started with a very rough 1975 FLH then applied their sign painting (and mechanical) skills to transform it into this very contemporary cruiser. Note the whitewall tires on spoked rims, paint instead of chrome on many parts, and the modern graphics.

Fiberglass bags were widened and the rear fender features a frenched license plate and taillight. Pinstripes and graphics are Lenny's own.

What the kids would call an old man's bike—big, slow, and comfortable like an old Buick. No one could stretch their imagination far enough to see the potential inherent in these big motorcycles.

The old Shovelhead engine has been rebuilt and now carries an Andrews H-grind camshaft for more power. Air cleaner and battery box are painted in pearl white to match the rest of the bike.

Adrian Newkirk started his project with a stretched, raked FXR frame, and then added a 39mm Wide Glide fork mounted in Arlen Ness billet triple trees. The dual-rail swingarm is from Arlen, too, as are the Taildragger fenders. The gas tank was stretched to match the longer frame.

All that has changed.

In recent years there are more and more Dressers on the streets, and more and more of them are being customized. Instead of adding widgets and accessories, the new breed of owner is removing things from the motorcycle. Donnie Smith and Drag Specialties were on the leading edge of this trend with the wonderful red and silver Dresser they introduced a few years ago.

Lowered, painted, and stripped of some bulk, the new Dressers are good looking bikes, with the essence of the design left intact and fewer distracting

The front fairing is a much-modified FXRT unit with hand-formed "lowers." Dual disc front brakes use Performance Machine calipers mounted to powder-coated lower legs. This long, radical ride rolls on Metzeler 18-inch tires mounted to spoked rims.

What separates Adrian's bike from similar machines are the details. Things like the hand-formed trim at the edges of the fenders and the taillight and license plate set into the rear fender.

lights and bezels to distract the viewer. Once again close to its customers, Harley-Davidson is cashing in on this trend with the new Road King (put your name on a list now for delivery some time in the next century) and before that the FLH Sport. FXRTs (a Dresser in my book) have suddenly reached Most Popular status and qualify as a good starting point for a wild customizing job, as evidenced by the work of both Arlen Ness and Donnie Smith. Older Shovelhead FLH bikes have become classic icons like some kind of two-wheeled '59 Cadillac.

Maybe it's the baby boomers getting older and going slower with more comfort. Whatever the reason, the big bikes are suddenly very, very popular and ripe for a variety of modifications. FXRTs can be stretched and slimmed to create a cruise missile for the highway—with a radar detector as standard equipment. FL series bikes need only to be slammed, painted, and trimmed of some windshield height to qualify as hot cruising material for cool riders. With the right "old" parts, Dressers can become nostalgia bikes, much like certain Softails. Stripped of all but the most essential gear and painted in a wild 1990s paint scheme, the bikes are as modern and zoomy as a stretched-out FXR.

The aftermarket companies have made it easier for riders to customize their big bikes with a series of new parts designed especially for them. The new catalogs list shorty windshields, lowering kits, FLH-style

headlight nacelles, and dual exhaust systems all designed for "Hogs." What was an old man's bike or the one reserved for long trips has become a neat way to get around on two wheels. Men and women who ride Dressers no longer need to apologize because their bike isn't a Softail or an FXR.

The bikes presented here are but the tip of the iceberg, the first wave of what is sure to be a brace of newly customized Dressers. The first bike is one of those FXRT highway bikes. A Dresser that's definitely not an FLH but is equally cool nonetheless. Two of the bikes are Shovelhead FLH bikes, but you couldn't find two similar bikes that look more different. One uses classic styling cues and a modern paint job for a look that's both traditional and unique, the other uses one-off sheet metal to create a new-wave design reminiscent of certain automobiles of the 1950s.

Consider these bikes an appetizer tray designed to whet your appetite for the full course of Dressers to follow in the next few years.

Next page, Doug's late-model FLT got the smooth and modern treatment with help from Cycle Fab. Note the FLH headlight nacelle, the mostly monochromatic paint job, and the additional fork rake.

5-Customs

In a Class by Themselves

There's no doubt, Harley-Davidson builds good-looking motorcycles. With certain modifications and paint, the factory bikes can be made to look even better—or at least less like the other Softails or FXRs on the street. Yet, there are certain limitations imposed by the parts themselves. No matter how much you modify an FXR, it's still an FXR. At some point, it becomes easier and less expensive to start from scratch rather than spend a tremendous amount of time and money modifying an existing motorcycle.

Much of the unique sheet metal on Wink Eller's bike is shaped from aluminum sheet, including the side panels, rear fender/seat pan, and the chain guard. The gas tank is a Sportster unit. This 80-cubic-inch Evo is designed to run in the open-wheeled, stock displacement class at both El Mirage and Bonneville. By running with and without nitrous, one bike can compete in two classes. Engine cases are from House of Horsepower, and the heads were ported by Jerry Branch. Carburetor is a Super G from S&S, and the exhaust is Wink's own.

For individuals who insist on only the best, or those who want to start their project with a clean piece of paper, there is the full custom motorcycle. Pick a frame from Arlen Ness or Tripoli or Drag Specialties or Custom Chrome. Now, go out and buy a motor at a swap meet or over the counter at your local dealer (not always easy to do) or have one built from aftermarket components. You need a transmission too, and will the primary drive be a chain or belt? How about the drive to the rear wheel?

Next, select the tank(s), fenders, wheels, and all the rest of the items on your list. Now, mock everything up in your shop, modify and alter certain parts to fit like they're supposed to, and then pull everything apart again for painting and plating. Finally, you get to assemble and ride your "new" motorcycle.

It ain't easy, and it certainly isn't cheap, but it does allow the builder a tremendous amount of freedom—freedom to put together a bike with exactly the characteristics and design he or she wants. Long and lean or short and fat, Softail or Hardtail, springer or hydraulic fork, what you want is what you get. Usually reserved for serious Harley fanatics and professional bike builders, the custom route is becoming more and more popular.

As the price of new Harley-Davidsons continues to rise, it becomes easier to justify the expense of building a bike from scratch. Expanded aftermarket offerings also make it more alluring to build this way by offering the potential builder a

Metzeler rear tire measures a wide 170/55x18 inches and connects by chain to a modified five-speed gear box.

larger parts bin to chose from.

Most of the bikes seen in this chapter were built by professionals like Donnie Smith or Dave Perewitz. They represent the pinnacle of custom bike design and assembly. These are full-on, "take no prisoners" custom motorcycles. If what the bike needs is a longer tank, then someone makes one. If the radius of the fender doesn't match the radius of the wheel, well someone modifies the fender until it does—or they make a fender from scratch.

Wink Eller used a Paughco Hardtail frame, FXR forks, some very nice hand-formed panels, and a NOS-equipped motor to create this wild red Bonneville bike. Spoked Akront rims measure 18 inches on both ends and Performance Machine calipers slow everything down.

The machines shown include blower bikes; long, stretched-out creations; short and stubby scoots; and a few Hardtails. Like I said earlier, with a true custom bike, you can have anything you want. Exotic or functional, it's all possible and it's probably represented here.

There's no skimping on parts. The hardware on these bikes is all top shelf. Most roll on wheels made from an aluminum rim mated to spokes cut from billet 6061 T6 aluminum. Brake calipers, too, have been cut from billet aluminum on computerized

The special Cycle Fab fabricated swingarm makes it possible to run a fat, 180x17-inch Metzeler tire and retain the belt drive. The FXR fender was widened to cover the new tire and modified to accept the flush-mount taillight. Wide tire and belt drive combination meant Dave spent a lot of time during the mock-up stage positioning the engine, transmission, and rear wheel.

Left, Mike Brown's very long orange custom is based on an Arlen Ness five-speed frame, a stroker motor, and some very special sheet metal. The front fender is a modified Sportster unit, the rear fender came from an FXR, and the gas tanks started life as 3-1/2-gallon Fat Bobs. The air dam is a "Hotop Special."

Unusual wheels and six piston calipers are the latest in high performance machinery from Performance Machine.

The fenders are Taildraggers from Arlen Ness, while the oil tank, primary cover, and chain guard have all been fabricated by Mal Ross. The idea was to keep this Shovelhead skinny, hence you see fender struts that wrap around slender fenders, the tapered FXR tank, Narrow Glide fork, and sectioned handlebars.

CNC equipment before being polished or chrome plated. The plumbing between the caliper and master cylinder is high-quality, braided stainless steel line.

Before these bikes are painted, the frames

Left, Not just any old Evo, this is an 89-cubic-inch stroker built from polished Delkron cases and an S&S bottom end, topped with painted and plated Harley-Davidson barrels and heads—all fed by a new Mikuni 42mm flat-slide carburetor.

and sheet metal parts are "molded" or smoothed out with filler so that all the seams and welds disappear, and the elaborate paint jobs go on a perfectly smooth surface.

The paint jobs themselves involve a number of steps. First the primer is applied, then the base coat followed by pearl or candy colors, and then the clear coat. Graphics are applied after the final color, unless the builder is after a special effect like ghost scallops (which are applied someplace in the middle of the candy coats). The finished paint job lies flat and perfect, without a flaw or ripple on an absolutely smooth surface. The perfection exhibited in these bikes—exemplified by the paint jobs—isn't an accident, it comes from careful planning, thorough

This 80-cubic-inch Shovelhead was completely rebuilt before being installed in the frame. Inside is an S&S bottom end, Wiseco pistons, and Andrews camshaft. Outside, it's brandywine paint combined with polished cam and rocker covers.

Right, this Mal Ross custom is based on a hardtail frame, Shovelhead engine, and some unusual body work. Note how the pipes run uphill at the same angle as the bars and how the air cleaner's shape mimics that of the gas tank.

To achieve a different look, Dave Perewitz used a wide-glide front end. Performance Machine supplied the 17x3-inch spun-aluminum front wheel which is mated to an Avon tire. Four-piston calipers are from PM as well.

Left, Dave's front fender is from a Fat Boy while the rear is a widened FLH unit modified to accept the flush-mount taillight. The rear fender was widened to straddle the 160x17-inch tire mounted to the Performance Machine aluminum rim.

Perewtiz's long purple Harley-Davidson gets its people-pleasing power from the Arlen Ness five-speed frame, wide-glide fork, one-off tank, and great magenta paint applied by the team of Perewitz and Perewitz.

Below, this Evo is a little unusual in that it breathes through an SU carburetor and ignites with a Morris magneto. Under all that chrome and glitter is a stroker motor with a 4-5/8-inch bottom end and 3-1/2-inch pistons from S&S. The guts are harbored in Delkron cases and topped by Harley-Davidson cylinders and heads.

The engine in Larry's sanitary ride is a balanced and blueprinted 80-cubic-inch Evo with Crane Cam, S&S Series-E carburetor, and Bub pipes. The powder-coated white engine wears limited chrome and dove-tails nicely with the motorcycle's overall design.

Right, Larry Page wanted a simple motorcycle, so he chose a Pro Street frame without extra stretch or rake (and no side covers), combined with an uncluttered 80-cubic-inch engine, simple sheet metal, and a clean paint job. Front and rear billet wheels are the new Viper design from Performance Machine. PM was chosen to supply the four-piston calipers as well.

Previous page right, the gas tank started as a Super Glide tank, though it's hard to recognize. Mr. Giggie at Departure Bike Works installed a flush-mount gas cap and stretched the tank 3 inches to better fit the frame.

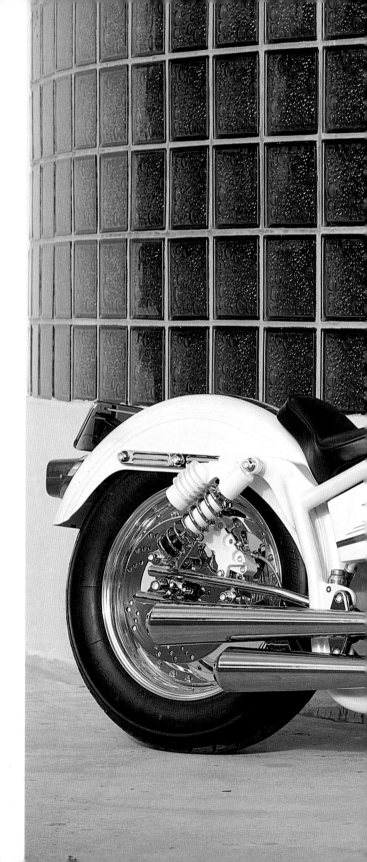

The old Shovelhead engine powers this chopper, but it's been rebuilt and equipped with some of the very latest in accessories—like a billet air cleaner and flamed points cover. Cases are polished, while the barrels and heads were chrome plated then painted red to match the bike.

Left, a true chopper needs all the right stuff, and this Arlen Ness special has it—a pre-Evo V-twin, a Hardtail frame with a short springer front end, a 21-inch spoked rim, no front fender, and ape-hanger handlebars. Arlen likes to mix the old with the new, thus we have a billet chain guard and grips, flamed derby cover, and new-wave floorboards.

Delkron cases form the foundation for this 80-cubic-inch mill. Cylinders and ported heads are from The Motor Company. The V-twin inhales through a Model B S&S carburetor with help from an S&S 561 camshaft and exhales into a pair of Bub pipes. A Primo belt drive carries power to the transmission. Note the one-off belt cover.

Right, the Five-Bs Pro Street bike is based on a stretched Tripoli hardtail frame, an 80-cubic-inch Evo engine, shortened Harley-Davidson fork tubes, and a stretched gas tank. Note the milled recesses on the calipers and brackets.

The same, only different. The Donnie Smith-built bike in the foreground mounts the blower on the right, uses flames sprayed over near-stock sheet metal, and a small fairing for a wild but conventional look. Steve Laugtug's bike however mounts the blower on the left and uses pastel colors and modern graphics sprayed over modified sheet metal for a very 1990s appearance.

preparation, and painstaking attention to detail during the application.

The finished machines are larger than life, often built by professionals for special customers or simply to highlight the shop's abilities—an expensive rolling billboard if you like. Elaborate and beautiful but functional as well, these bikes do run. In fact they roar with the bellow of modified V-twins built with that same "take no prisoners" attitude used on the rest of the bike.

A feast for the eyes and ears, these bikes provide inspiration for all the riders who haven't gotten that far yet. As a long, orange creation roars down main street Daytona, a hundred heads turn and at least half of those heads wish and promise that "some day, I'm going to have one of those."

HARLEY-DAVIDSON

ALLAN GIRDLER

AND

JEFF HACKETT

INTRODUCTION

My hobby is vintage racing, my mount is a 1970 Harley-Davidson XR-750 (details in chapter 8 but don't go there yet), and my transportation from home to track and back is a pickup truck.

At every other gas stop, or so it seems, I'll be pumping and somebody, employee or customer, will notice the bike and the labels and ask, "Harley-Davidson? When did Harley get into racing?"

"Oh," I say in as polite a tone as I can muster, "about 1908."

True fact, as we'll see in chapter 2.

Harley-Davidson, the brand, the product, and the legend, is known and admired around the world. Kids of all ages and nationalities wave if a Harley is in motion and stop to talk if it's not. (In case any Norwegian, Danish, Swedish, or Finnish moms wonder who taught their kids to say "Harley-Davidson is Number One" in English, it was me, riding an FLH to North Cape, Europe's northernmost landfall.) However, just because nearly everybody knows the name and the badge and the motorcycle doesn't mean they know the history.

It's a history worth knowing because the facts reinforce the legend: Four men with little more than grit and talent founded a company that rules its field nearly a century later. Its current success was wrested from near disaster; the product is—what the founders intended—as good a value for the money as can be found in our current culture; and in today's throwaway economy what you get now is a whole lot like what your father and his father got years ago.

Harley-Davidson history is a collection of stories, capturing the changing times. There are enough technical innovations to delight the world's motorheads, while at the same time there are people, make that heroes and heroines, who would make even Hollywood or the History Channel stop and take notice.

This is a short, concise history. Not all the facts or models are included here nor are they supposed to be. Instead, this is a history of the highlights, done so the reader will know why and how Harley-Davidson became the icon it is today.

—Allan Girdler

Author Allan Girdler (no shades) with a group of Americans at the FIM International Rally at Epernay, France in 1999. That's Allan's trusty XR-750 painted with a flag in the foreground. *Eric Corlay*

CHAPTER 1

WORKING ON THE RAILROAD

1 9 0 3

Now that Harley-Davidson is a world-class success story, an American icon, and the only survivor of motorcycling's pioneering past, now that we can afford the luxury of hindsight, it's safe to ask an unsettling question: Did The Motor Company, as the folks at H-D headquarters refer to the firm, become the one American motorcycle maker that lived while 200-plus rivals died because Harley's founders were machinists and toolmakers rather than bicycle guys?

Although this machine was assembled years after H-D went into business, for display it is labeled 1903 and 1904 because it has parts from both those years. Unlike most motorcycles of the time, this bike was assembled starting with the engine, which was fitted to the center of the oversized frame, with the bicycle pedals added on. Next, the wheels were fixed solidly in the frame, front and back. And if you look really closely, you'll see that the lever controlling the tension of the drive belt against the pulleys is linked to a pedal that does the same thing. There were times riders needed both hands on the grips and times when they needed both feet on the ground, so this preclutch control gave riders a choice. *Courtesy Harley-Davidson Archives*

Let's start at the beginning. The inventors of the motorcycle were two men who were working independently around 1868 or maybe 1869. One was an American named Sylvester Roper who lived near Boston. The other was a French inventor, Louis Perreaux, who put a steam engine aboard a pedal-powered bicycle, just then patented in 1868 by Pierre and Earnest Michaux. Roper didn't bother with pedals or patents or with keeping records, but both machines worked, or so the sketchy records claim, but neither the world, the bicycle, nor steam power was advanced enough to allow for a second act.

Fifteen or so years later, after Otto Daimler built a sort-of motorcycle as a mobile test bed for his internal combustion engine, the world was infatuated with the safety bicycle, with pedals, and pneumatic tires. Bicycle racing was a major sport, and somebody built a lumbering device with an engine, two wheels, and a windbreaker, to be ridden in front of bicycles so the riders wouldn't have to fight the air. (Yes, they were drafting 70 years before the stock-car crowd invented the art.) Meanwhile, scores of bright and ambitious chaps saw how logical it was to mount a gas engine on a bicycle, and many of these individuals went into the motorcycle business. Indian, the best of that breed, was the joint product of an engineering genius, the first man to make a reliable pacer (as the draft-breakers were called), and a champion bicycle racer who already owned a thriving bicycle factory.

At the same time, in Milwaukee, Wisconsin, there were three brothers, Arthur, William, and Walter Davidson. Milwaukee was a railroad town, and the brothers were members of the skilled craftsman class: Arthur was a pattern maker, William a toolmaker and fabricator, and Walter an apprentice machinist.

Arthur and his pal William Harley, who worked as a fitter in a bicycle plant, were bicycle enthusiasts, using them for transportation and hunting and fishing expeditions. It seemed logical to them that a bicycle with a motor would get them farther, faster.

Both young men had mechanical aptitude and they had friends who could help, including one named Ole Evinrude (yes, *that* Evinrude), so they began studying and then building single-cylinder engines that could be bolted to a bicycle, or so they hoped.

Besides having a keen interest and aptitude for things mechanical, Harley and the Davidsons had something else in their favor—they were railroad guys. People form lifelong habits and impressions from where they first work. They adopt the culture around them. The railroad culture, back then especially, centered around the work ethic. The train had to get there. On time. Intact. Railroads weren't sport; they were real life.

The founders, seen here in an official photo from 1910. From the left, William A. Davidson, the older brother who ran the plant; Walter Davidson, natural rider and company president; Arthur Davidson, salesman and organizer; and William Harley, the chief engineer. As the poses and suits indicate, by this time the founders were grown men and owners of a successful business. *Courtesy Harley-Davidson Archives*

With a strong work ethic ingrained in them, around 1900 or 1901, Harley and Arthur Davidson began building engines and testing them. In 1902, or so legend claims, Walter was literally beneath a locomotive on the Missouri, Kansas and Texas Railroad in Parsons, Kansas, when he got a message inviting him to come home and ride the motorized bicycle brother Arthur and friend Harley had been building. (Not to spoil the story, but he also was heading for Milwaukee to attend brother William's wedding.)

What he found when he got there was a complete set of motorcycle parts rather than a motorcycle, and the deal was he could ride it when he had put it together. (He did, but not then and there, because the first motorcycle Harley and the Davidsons completed didn't actually run until the spring of 1903.)

Here's where the railroad training began to pay off. The engine ran well enough and long enough to make clear to them the inadequacy of the bicycle-scale frame the builders were using. So they went, as the cliché puts it, back to the drawing board. They made a larger engine, which would produce not only more power but would do so with less stress.

And they made a new frame, larger and with stronger (and heavier) tubing. Not only that, they placed the engine in the middle and looped the frame around and below the engine. If you look at the other pioneers from the turn of the century, you'll see bicycles, with the pedal and crank in the center and the engine added.

Hell for stout, as the saying goes. Beyond that the prototype motorcycle was as basic as could be. The wheels were solidly mounted in the frame and the

WILLIAM HARLEY, CHIEF ENGINEER

Serendipity may have played a part, but the major factor in H-D's early success was William Harley. On the one hand, Harley stepped out of the limelight. It was the Davidson brothers, three to one, who voted to call the infant manufacturing operation Harley-Davidson, on the grounds that it sounded better. (Davidson-Harley works as well as, oh, Royce-Rolls or Johnson-Ivor, eh?)

On the other hand, Harley did not hide his natural mechanical ability. He had enough to know he didn't know what he needed to know, so later, in 1903, when he was 23 years old and a grown man gainfully employed, Harley enrolled in the engineering school at the University of Wisconsin at Madison.

To appreciate this, move back a century. Only a tiny fraction of the population went to college then. Harley wasn't well-to-do, nor was his family. He worked his way through, waiting tables for a fraternity as well as doing after-school mechanical projects for firms near the school.

Commitment is the word that fits here. To top it off, while working his way through school, Harley provided Arthur Davidson (who was home in the family's back yard building two more motorcycles to order) with engineering and other practical advice.

In his senior year, when the partners and the industry knew the solidly mounted front wheels were fine on bicycles but not with engines added, Harley designed a front suspension—leading links controlled by coil springs—that not only was the best in the field at the time, but was good enough to serve for the next 40 years (and it would even later come back as the nostalgic Springer version of the Softail). The leading-link design was also licensed out for use by European factories.

Harley wasn't an innovator or a creative genius. Rather, he made sure something worked before it was adopted and that the product was good value even if it wasn't flashy. He viewed his work as being for the long run, and the company's long run is in large part due to the tradition he established.

---

forks. There was one speed, well, perhaps it's more accurate to say drive was direct, with a leather belt between the engine pulley and the rear wheel pulley, with a lever the rider moved to tighten or loosen the belt's grip. There were no lights or any road equipment as we know it now. To start, the rider pedaled up to speed, set the controls for the carburetor (the design of which had occupied a lot of Harley's time and drew on Evinrude's advice), and pulled the belt tight enough to turn the engine. When things went right, the engine ran and the pedals served as footrests.

What mattered in the motorcycling world of 1903 was that the prototype worked. Harley and the Davidsons knew how to make a motorcycle.

What came next is a matter of minor debate. Some accounts hold that the original idea was simply for William Harley and Arthur Davidson to build a motorcycle for their own use and that the business began when other people saw the prototype, knew it was a superior machine, and wanted one like it.

The other version, which seems more likely based on the time and money the pals put into the project, was that at some point between the first drawings and the first ride, they realized they could compete. This was an age of opportunity, so they took it one step at a time, and the Harley-Davidson Motor Company was born.

CHAPTER 2

EARLY PRODUCTION

1904 – 1908

When actual production of Harley-Davidsons began in 1904, the fledgling firm was very much a family operation. Walter Davidson quit the railroad shop to be H-D's only full-time employee, working in a shed in the Davidson back yard, while Arthur kept his day job and helped at night, along with some part-time workers. Not only that, but early finances were eased by support from a well-to-do maternal uncle.

But one of the best early stories has to be about the badge: the Harley-Davidson Motor Company bar and shield. The Davidson boys had a maiden aunt with a talent for art, and the legend says Aunt Janet did the design, which has gone on to rank with Ford's script or McDonald's arch, along with applying gold stripes to the black paint used on those first machines. There have since been mutterings that the badge fable is just that,

The first Harley engines were based on French design. There is no mechanical linkage for the intake valve because it's opened and closed by atmospheric pressure, but these bikes do have a control allowing riders to bypass the muffler on the open road or to be quiet in town— one reason this model was nicknamed the Silent Gray Fellow.

but there's such a thing as researching a story too far, so from this soapbox, Aunt Janet gets the credit.

The first Harleys were as basic as they could be. The designers were, after all, new to the business and not even the veterans really understood just how internal combustion took place.

Harley's single-cylinder engine displaced about 25 cubic inches, making it larger than the average for the day. (The details here are vague because the builders made more running changes than they made notes.) The intake valve was above the exhaust valve, both offset from the piston, with the space between them forming most of the combustion chamber. This system, known as intake over exhaust (IOE) or pocket valve, was the conventional design of that time.

Those first singles had an automatic intake valve, meaning that the valve was pulled open when the piston went down, then pushed shut when compression began and held shut through the power and exhaust strokes, then pulled open again on the intake stroke. This system, along with the camshaft and lobe for the exhaust, did the job for as long as engine rpm was measured in the hundreds.

201

Oil and gas tanks were attached to the frame above the engine, so feed was by gravity, a method still in use today for fuel tanks in all but the most exotic motorcycles.

Pioneer lubrication came to have a worse reputation than it deserved. The early engines used roller bearings, ran at low speeds, and didn't need a lot of oil, so the factory calculated the need and designed the drip feed to suit. There was also a pump for the rider to operate when the engine was putting out extra power, such as when climbing a hill. What made this look bad later was the term *total loss,* which conjured up the image of oil going to the engine, being whirled around inside the crankcase, and dumped on the ground. How it sounds isn't how it worked, but the name stuck.

The first motorcycles from the backyard shed were basic, meaning no lights or horn, a seat for operator only, one speed with some variation allowed by the belt drive, a bicycle-style coaster brake in the rear hub, no brake in front, and wheels rigidly mounted to the frame and forks.

Some of this simplicity was to keep costs down, but just as much was because the motorcycle idea was new, and the practical parts were still being developed. The carburetor was just then becoming a working instrument, for example, and the controls were intricate assemblies of levers, pivots, cranks, crevices, and rods, because the creative likes of Glenn Curtiss were just then working out the Bowdoin cable and the twist control.

Early production Harley-Davidsons were very basic machines, as in one cylinder, one seat, and no lights. But this 1910 Model 6—so designated because 1910 was the sixth year of H-D production—has a front suspension designed by William Harley and a tensioner for its belt drive.

WALTER DAVIDSON, ENDURANCE RACER

There was another major development and another happy accident in 1908.

As it happened, William Harley was a good rider, and so was Arthur Davidson, while big brother William enjoyed the business and the convenience but never really rode much just for fun.

But Walter Davidson was, as they say in baseball, a natural.

Motorcycles, make that motor vehicles, had a lot to prove early in the century. They scared horses, ran off

Walter Davidson wore an expression of honest pride after he'd won the national enduro and put H-D into the headlines if not on the map. This is 1908, so Walter's mount has the leading-link front suspension that would be used for the next 40 years. Notice all the control rods, links, pivots, and levers it took to connect man and machine before the twist grip and Bowdoin cable were invented. You can also see that the motorcycling attire of 1908 was much different from today's. With increased speeds, a coat, tie, and cap would not be practical motorcycling gear in the modern era. *Courtesy Harley-Davidson Archives*

roads, made noise, and broke down, which was the major drawback. Not for nothing did George Hendee and Oscar Hedstrom, the powers behind Indian, invite the local press to Killer Hill so the Indian prototype could climb it with ease. This made front-page news, and Indian was famous overnight.

Because the motorcycle had something to prove, racing was as much proving ground and public display of confidence as it was sport. In 1908 the national club, the Federation of American Motorcyclists (FAM), sanctioned and organized a national championship endurance run. Endurance meant just that; the club set a nearly impossible two-day schedule, and the riders came as close as they could.

Half of the 84 entrants were out by the end of the first day. At the end of the second day, Walter Davidson had a perfect score. It was so perfectly perfect that the club gave him five bonus points for a perfect-plus finish.

The next week, Walter ran in the FAM economy run where his Model 5 single returned 188, yes, one-eight-eight miles per gallon. This was on a stock machine; stock in the sense that at that time all Harleys were assembled by hand and checked out before hitting the road.

In the long run, Walter's skill made the brand famous while his interest and enthusiasm ensured that the product would be what the motorcycle nut wanted, even before the buyer knew it for himself. Later, when H-D did form a team, Walter was in favor: Just because he didn't race for money didn't mean he objected to professionals. And he was known for being honest and generous, in an era where the fix was known and the handshake often wasn't enough.

What Harley and the Davidsons could do was make motorcycles that worked. They made and delivered two such machines in 1904 and six more in 1905. They doubled the size of the building and the crew and in 1906 produced about 50 machines, this time with a twist-grip throttle and a larger engine.

During this time, bicycle enthusiasts went racing with their motorcycles just as they'd done with the human-powered two-wheelers. While Harley-Davidson didn't have a factory team or production racer, historian Jerry Hatfield has turned up a letter, dated late 1905, in which sales manager Arthur Davidson told a prospective buyer that a Harley had covered 15 miles on a track in Chicago in 19:02 minutes, proving that the Harley-Davidson was the fastest single-cylinder on the market.

In 1906 there came the first option, gray paint with red trim. Possibly because good manners are noticed, H-D supplied efficient mufflers, and the model was known as the Silent Gray Fellow. (Imagine how that would go over now, when even motorhomes are tagged Marauder or Predator.)

William Harley delivered his leading-link suspension for the 1907 models. To go with increased production and staff, the partnership became a corporation. Harley was appointed chief engineer, Arthur Davidson was sales manager, Walter was the firm's first president, and William Davidson quit his railroad job to become plant manager.

Seldom have there been better examples of the right people in the right place at the right time. Just as William Harley matched the profile for the best engineer, so did Arthur turn out to be a canny and effective sales manager and the right man to build a dealer network. And by the time William Davidson took over the plant, he was a foreman in the railroad shops. He was also a large and hearty man who could do the work his men were doing, and at a time when might could settle the question of right, he was big enough to do that part too.

In 1908, with the development of differences in the models, The Motor Company needed a form of identification. At first, they used a simple number system. The 1908 models were called Model 4 because they were produced during the fourth year of model production. The following year, when there was a choice between battery or magneto to power the ignition, the Model 5 had a battery and the 5A used a magneto.

Although straightforward in the beginning, H-D's identification system would get more confusing, as you will see in later chapters.

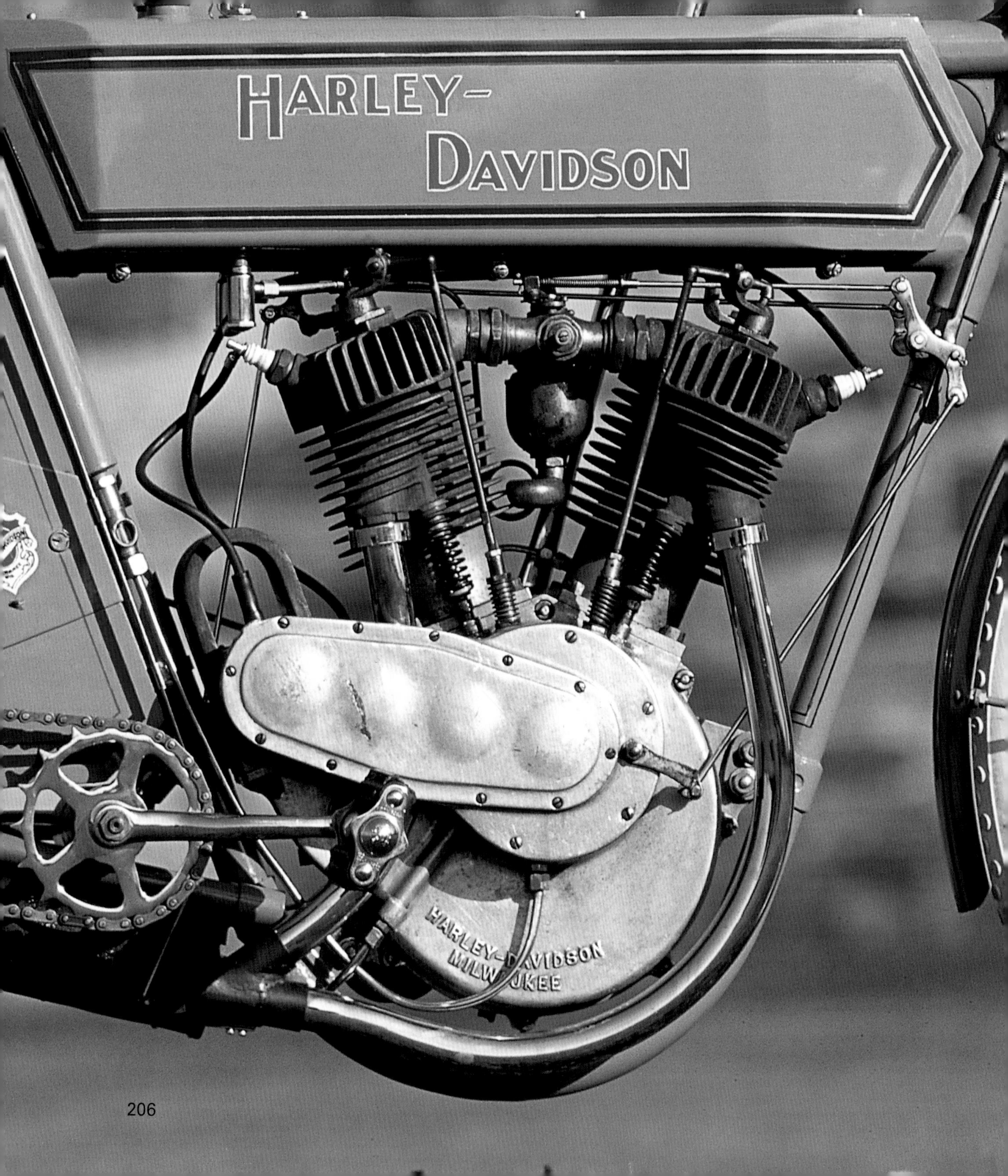
HARLEY-
DAVIDSON

V-TWINS RULE

1 9 0 9 – 1 9 2 9

Harley-Davidson's most enduring tradition, the narrow-angle V-twin, not only wasn't an H-D invention, but Milwaukee's version was the firm's first failure.

The idea of two cylinders set at an angle above a shared crankshaft was logical. A glance at a bicycle's conventional frame shows that once you set a single cylinder at the bottom of the frame's vee, you might as well use two cylinders, which builders began doing very early.

Researchers have found some hints of an early V-twin in the Harley archives dating back to 1907, but the first official version came in 1909, when a twin, with the cylinders fore-and-aft, inline, and with both connecting rods on the same crankpin, was added to the choice of singles with battery or magneto.

The twin lasted less than a year. The model found buyers, but what hadn't been reckoned with was that the

H-D's first successful V-twin appeared in 1911. The V-twin logic, the perfect fit of the narrow vee within the frame, is obvious here, but the real secret is that pair of pushrods—from the camshaft sited below the vee to the intake valve rockers atop the head. This made it possible for the V-twin to start via the pedals and increased engine speed.

added power, an estimated 7 brake horsepower, versus 5 for the single, was too much for the drive belt to hold, plus the twin's automatic inlet valves limited engine speed and made the engine almost impossible to start.

H-D did make progress on other fronts, however; William Harley got a patent on a two-speed rear hub, the belt control was improved, and lights became an option, either electric via generator and battery or with acetylene gas, produced by dropping pellets into a tank where the pellets dissolved in water and became a gas that was piped to the headlight and burned (if that sounds like a bother, the batteries of the day were even more so).

The big news for 1911 was the return of the V-twin, with the same displacement but with a camshaft lobe and gear for the intake valves. It was a markedly improved engine, especially now that the two-speed hub had a speed to cruise and one to climb with.

In 1912, the frame was revised to allow suspending the seat on a sliding post, which soaked up the big bumps, and in 1914 came a starting system that allowed removal of the pedals and chain, the last vestige of the bicycle ancestor. The Harley term was *step-start,* which is more elegant than *kick-start,* eh?

The next generation, roughly 1916 through 1929, saw some remarkable contrasts. We'll call this a generation because there is a constant, the use of the intake-over-exhaust (IOE) engine, the basic idea of which was seen on that first H-D engine. There were detail changes and major improvements and variations, for instance the eight-valve, fully overhead-valve racing conversions built atop the IOE cases. And there was a line of economy-model singles with side valves; cheaper to build and run.

While the major engine design was retained, there was a stream of improvements, the three-speed transmission and the foot-controlled clutch, for two. There were electric lights with battery and generator, and the stripped loss-leaders. The model line expanded until there were standard, sports, and commercial machines, along with cargo and delivery rigs.

With this expansion came the need for identification, in the plant and in dealerships. The old way, the Model 5 and 5A, didn't tell enough of the story.

By 1915 when this Model 11-J was made, the Harley V-twin came with step-start—no more pedaling down the road—a headlight, a taillight, a luggage rack, and a sliding post for the seat to absorb the worst of the bumps, and, oh, yes, the tire people had discovered that mixing white rubber with a dash of carbon black made the tires much more durable.

This 1917 V-twin introduced a major theme in motorcycle history—the cut-down. This machine, a J or JD, has a single-cam road engine, and the step-start has been shifted to the right. But notice there's no muffler or lights, and the fenders have been trimmed back. Such cut-down machines became the fashion when the factory fitted all the extras.

The new way began with letters, seemingly chosen in roughly alphabetical order: the Model E followed the Model D, with the W coming after the U and the V—except that the E was a big twin, the D had been a middleweight, and so was the W, while the U and the V were big twins.

Letters were added, also in random fashion. The basic H-D engine, the 61-cubic-inch IOE twin, was the Model J. If it came with magneto, it was the F. A J enlarged to 74 cubic inches was the JD. Late in the series, the engine got a second camshaft: the 61-cubic-inch engine was then the JH, and the 74 cubic inch the JDH. The basic engine with sports extras was the JL.

The joke now is that only two people understand Harley's system; one is retired, and the other is dead. So you can memorize the code, but you can't break it.

Factory racing was serious business. This 1921 two-cam began as a J engine, but each cylinder gets its own two-lobe camshaft, and the special frame uses the engine cases as a bridge. There's no frame tube below the engine, so the engine sits closer to the ground. No brakes, of course.

Completely different from other Harleys, the WJ Sport used a fore-and-aft twin-cylinder engine with an enclosed drive chain and girder forks. The example pictured here is an unrestored version built in 1921. The WJ Sport was quiet, efficient, and a sales flop that was dropped from the catalog after 1923.

This sounds paradoxical, but as motorcycles became more reliable and useful, motorcycling became more sport and less transportation. (To simplify, as soon as all motorcycles could get there from here, the issue became which one could get there first.)

Promoters came up with spectacles, huge, banked board ovals allowing speeds well above 100 miles per hour. They provided close, dangerous, and thrilling races, which drew the crowds and that meant everybody who picked up a newspaper on Monday knew which brand had won on Sunday.

Modest mention of private success was no longer enough, so in 1914 Harley-Davidson fielded a racing team, matching Indian and Excelsior. They raced souped and stripped J-powered specials and later had four-valve tops for the J crankcases; these were called Eight Valves because there were four for each cylinder.

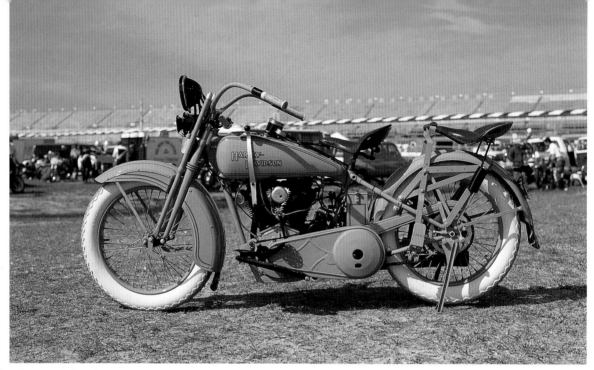

By 1927 the J-series, represented here by a 74-cubic-inch JD, used a pair of rounded fuel tanks slung over the frame tube, deeply valanced fenders for weather protection, a three-speed transmission with hand shift and foot clutch, and even a sprung seat for a passenger.

The big news for 1928 was the first use of a front brake, seen here on a JD that also has crash bars—the hoops outboard of the frame's front downtube. The left-side tank contains oil, delivered to the crankcase by working the plunger handle, just visible on top of the tank.

One of racing's recurring problems appeared now for the first time. The competition machines became faster and more specialized and less like road machines, all at once. Enthusiasts could ride to the races, but they couldn't ride and race the same motorcycle.

The board tracks were spectacular and dangerous. Make that fatal, all too often, with the victims spectators as well as riders. This was an easy target for the tabloid press—they had such even back then, before the line at the check-out counter—and professional motorcycle racing became as much show business as sport.

The benefit, perhaps the only benefit, was that the builders and tuners developed and acquired technical skill and knowledge at an accelerated rate.

Then came World War I and some canny moves by Harley's founders. The War Department (later known

Sidecars were still popular in 1928, and the JD frame came ready for the outfit to be bolted on. The black gadget below the headlight was known for years as an electrical signal, because back then if it didn't have a bell like a trumpet or trombone, it wasn't a horn. And the canister below the signal is the toolbox.

As racing got faster, the rules called for smaller engines in hopes of reducing speed, while the racers got better at getting more from less. This is an early Model B with a 21-cubic-inch single with overhead valves (OHV). It's rigged for short-track racing with no brakes, no suspension, the gear lever moved to the right so the rider has clearance to put his foot down, and a brace—the taped black thing in front of the seat that the rider wedges his right leg against. These machines were known as Pea-shooters because the engine went pop-pop-pop.

as the Department of Defense) saw the motorcycle as a useful addition and ordered thousands of examples.

At that time, Indian was the sales leader. The financial wizards who'd taken over from Hendee and Hedstrom took out the dealers, whom they saw as middlemen, and sold all the bikes they could make directly to the military.

The military used the motorcycle almost exclusively for courier and traffic control, so the actual machines were the standard road models, F- and J-series twins in Harley-Davidson's case.

Neither factory's production was reduced, except that H-D continued to supply the civilian market through its

BLACK JACK PERSHING VERSUS PANCHO VILLA: MOTORCYCLES GO TO WAR

General John J. Pershing, nicknamed "Black Jack" because he commanded African American troops early in his career, was a World War I hero and by the evidence in all the pictures, a man of military bearing and stern demeanor—Old Guard right to the ramrod-straight core. He was an unlikely pioneer, at best.

In 1916 General Francisco "Pancho" Villa, who'd been on the losing side of one of the several revolutions Mexico was having at the time, took to raiding small towns on the U.S. side of the border. Villa was a popular loser, and the Mexican authorities couldn't cope, so they gave permission for the U.S. Army to pursue Villa and his men on whichever side of the line Villa was.

Pershing led 20,000 troops into Mexico, and with the troops came motorcycles: Harley-Davidsons, Indians, and a few Excelsiors, all big twins and most fitted with sidecars.

This was the first recorded incidence of motorcycles in combat, although the police had seen the uses of two-wheeled pursuit very early in motorized history. And as it happened, this was nearly the only time motorcycles were used in actual combat.

Pershing's men were free to experiment, and they fitted the sidecars with machine guns. The rigs made a good platform, and the timing, when compared to the time it took to haul a machine gun and cart with mules and then rig it for fighting, was in the cycle's favor.

Perhaps the best part of the story is that Villa's soldiers also had motorcycles, and there's a surviving snapshot of Pancho himself, grinning like motorcycle nuts always have, about to leap on an Indian's kick-start pedal. If you are one of those novelists who mingle fact with fiction, next time have Black Jack and Pancho motocrossing across Sonora, Indian versus Harley.

In real life, this never happened. What happened was the armies learned that motorcycles were faster than mules and horses but that riding and shooting at the same time wasn't like sitting on a horse and slashing infantry with a sword. So as Villa managed to elude Pershing's larger force, the military learned motorcycles were better used for courier duty than as motorized cavalry.

But Harley-Davidson took advantage of photo opportunities and showed the public lots of shots of Harleys in the army. What the record doesn't show is Black Jack on a Harley; while his troops piloted cycles of various makes, there's no evidence he ever rode one himself.

normal outlets, so when the war was over and people had cash, time, and a taste for adventure, Harley had a dealer network, and Indian didn't. Harley took the sales lead and kept it until Indian went out of production 35 years later.

During the 1920s H-D concentrated on the J-series twins, with some smaller singles for commercial buyers and some experiments such as the W-series Sport, a fore-and-aft twin smaller than the Js. It was quieter, easier to start and ride—but not enough people wanted a practical motorcycle, and it didn't look right. The model was dropped, and it took H-D management a long time to try any other radical notions.

CHAPTER 4

SIDEVALVE SURVIVORS

1928 – 1935

The his may be an unheralded virtue, but something must be said in favor of the person who can openly and cheerfully adopt an idea not invented here.

That's pretty much what William Harley and the Davidsons did in 1928.

The intake-over-exhaust (IOE) engines did a good job through the 1920s. The singles had become twins; the twins grew and developed. There was a special run of high-performance J engines (the 500-series), and the J lower end was used for the four-valve racers.

It was all to the good, except that Indian had gone to sidevalve engines, flatheads as they said then, and the sidevalve Indians were as powerful as the IOE Harleys, plus they made less noise, needed less maintenance, and cost less to make.

William Harley and the engineering staff knew this and designed new engines. They considered overhead

The V engines had four single-lobe camshafts in the gearcase (as H-D-speak terms it) in the right-side engine case half. Each lobe opened one valve, which was complicated but precise. The heat shield on the rear exhaust pipe of this 1934 VLD, the sporting 74, is a later addition.

valves, which were being used on English motorcycles and by U.S. car makers, Chevrolet notably, but OHV engines are more complex and cost more to make. So H-D took the practical approach, looking at the amount of performance needed, and made the largest, least-expensive engine that would deliver the goods.

To this practical approach, Harley-Davidson added its own principle, which is to not make all the moves at the same time. So while the J-series twin continued in production, along with the singles and the competition machines in 1928, H-D introduced a new line of middleweights, powered by 45-cubic-inch sidevalve V-twins. The new model was designated D. It had a front brake, which H-D also added to the J-series that year, along with a four-tube exhaust and dual headlights. The D's engine joined the gearbox via the primary drive. It had four one-lobe camshafts in an arc below the valves, and its generator was mounted vertically at the engine's left front, parallel to the front cylinder.

Because of its configuration, Indian fans called the new machine the three-cylinder Harley. The D received so much abuse because it was a direct competitor of the Indian Scout, also a 45-cubic-inch sidevalve V-twin. By no coincidence, H-D and Indian had tried smaller V-twins, the Sport and the original Scout, respectively, and learned that the large and powerful middleweights sell better than small and thrifty ones.

For the 1930 model year, the D was retained and the J-series 61s and 74s were replaced by the V-series, 74-cubic-inch sidevalves that came with different stages of tune but in the same displacement.

Harley-Davidson's teapot had acquired its very own tempest.

H-D's introduction of the sidevalve engine came as quite a shock. For generations Harley fans had argued with Indian fans over the merits of the intake over exhaust versus the sidevalve, and Pow! one day H-D took the Indian path. Some Harley folks felt abandoned and proclaimed the J engine to be the best motorcycle engine ever made, and 60 years later you can still find some vintage owners who'll tell you exactly that.

No one could dispute the fact that both the D-series and V-series bikes had serious flaws when they first went into production. Revisions were made to the engine and frame, and the factory organized what amounted to a recall campaign long before such things were common. All the troubles, though, were worth the effort. The big sidevalve

The all-new 1930 V series looked more familiar, with its paint scheme and dual headlights carried over from the 1929 J-series. But the sidevalve, 74-cubic-inch engine and three-speed transmission (plus reverse in case you fitted a factory-backed sidecar, as seen here) shared no parts.

1930 HARLEY-DAVIDSON
45 cu.in. RACER
MOTOR NUMBER 30 DLD 5621

BUILT IN 1932 BY: *Harry Stalter Sr.*
H-D DEALER SINCE 1905, HOU., TX

RIDDEN BY: *Bill Anderson* #8 HOU., TX
1932-1940: WON TEXAS STATE T.T.
CHAMPIONSHIP 1934: POCHILO RANCH COURSE,
WACO, TEXAS, AGAINST 80 cu. in. MACHINES

1937 GALVESTON, TEXAS, BEACH TIME TRIALS
SET 45 cu. in. TIME AT 98 PLUS M.P.H.

BOUGHT BY: *Ricky Roux* BEAUMONT, TX IN 1940
WHO ENJOYED MANY WINS. RICKY JOINED
THE AIR FORCE 1941. LEFT BIKE WITH
Woody Lione Sr. #0 WHO RODE IT BEFORE & AFTER
WORLD WAR II WITH GOOD RESULTS
RICKY RETURNED: RODE & RETIRED IT IN 1947.
THE BIKE SUFFERED SERIOUS DAMAGE IN TWO
FLOODS AND WENT AS JUNK TO AUSTRALIA.
IN 1990, WOODY LOCATED AND BOUGHT
IT BACK FOR $3,750. HAND MADE MAGNESIUM
PISTONS AND MANY OTHER PARTS NOT AVAILABLE
2,000 HOURS

Racing was saved during the depths of the Great Depression by motorcycles such as this 1930 DLD—the *D* representing the 45-cubic-inch sidevalve V-twin that ushered in the H-D Flathead era, with *DL* standing for sports tune. Seen here as restored in 1992, this DLD was raced in TT events, a pre-motocross off-road contest. It's been stripped of lights and mufflers, and the front fender has been moved to the rear while the rear fender has been thrown away.

By 1933 the V-series, represented here by a VL, the standard customer model, had acquired its own look, with more graceful tanks and fenders and some extraordinary paint schemes. The sidevalve, 74-cubic-inch engine and gearbox are separate, each mounted on the frame and joined by a primary chain and housing.

The VL's rocker clutch pedal is just above the floorboard, while the hand shifter is located by a gate on the fuel tank. The springer forks don't have shock absorption yet, so the knobs on the sliders outboard of the fork springs are tensioned to keep the bounces under control.

engines were reliable. In 1930 H-D sold the plain V, the VL (the most popular version, which had a higher compression ratio), and the VM or VLM, the only difference in the latter being the magneto ignition. (Even then there were those who didn't trust motorcycle batteries.)

The V models were about 100 pounds heavier than the Js had been. They also were lower and had more power. Performance was close to equal with the JDH, except that a VL could hold top speed longer. The V and D were contemporary as well, with foot clutch, hand shift, and three speeds. For the 1932 model year reverse was added, mostly for the benefit of sidecar operators. However, the major news in 1932—aside from the collapse of the world's economy—was that the 45's generator was remounted, horizontally this time, and the frame was reworked, changing the model designation from D to R.

These were tough times, as the Great Depression got worse, and some extreme measures were taken.

Several years earlier, H-D had offered single-cylinder models, either sidevalve or overhead valve (OHV). They were offered at home and sent overseas, where practical machines were more in demand, especially when Harley-Davidson was a major exporter.

The models didn't sell and the singles were dropped from the catalog, but in 1932, when any sale was a plus, the company hauled out the parts for the models they hadn't sold or serviced, and reverse-shipped, brought back stocks from overseas, and reintroduced the single, with a 21-cubic-inch sidevalve engine called the Model B (yup, same as the much-more-famous 1932 Ford). At $195 it was the cheapest

The Model D with its vertical generator, was mocked as the "three-cylinder" Harley-Davidson. The Indian people love to tease.

The styling of the D was essentially identical to the Model V. Check the generator side and you'll know right away.

Harley-Davidson ever, and something close to 1,000 were assembled and presumably sold. Not much help, but surely better than letting the parts rust away.

The economic depression also led to the collapse of professional racing. Harley-Davidson was losing money, Indian was living day-to-day, and Excelsior had quit the motorcycle business. No one could afford to buy or race the specialized and exotic 500-cc machines that had been contesting the national events.

In an attempt to keep motorcycle racing alive in 1934, the American Motorcyclist Association, backed by Harley and Indian, drew up plans to make racing affordable. The

The 45-cubic-inch R series, which replaced the D models in 1932, got a new frame, with room for the generator to be horizontal at the front of the cases. The R machines—such as this 1934 RL—were junior big twins, so to speak, and could be bought with options including the fringed buddy seat, luggage rack, case guards, and brilliant paint schemes.

Looks can deceive. For 70 years, 1929 through 1999, Harley's big twins used two tank halves fitted to look like one tank. The left side of this 1934 VLD holds gas and oil, the latter delivered by the plunger pump aft of the gas cap. And yes, there are two keys, one for lights, the other for the ignition.

JOE PETRALI, CHAMPION RACER

Joe Petrali was a racer who set a record that not only will stand for all time but shows just how out-of-balance and unsporting racing had become in the depths of the Depression.

In the 1935 season, Joe Petrali won every national championship race. Every one.

To some degree this happened because in 1935 there was one factory with a racing team, Harley-Davidson, and that team consisted of one man, Joe Petrali.

These facts, however, don't give Petrali his due.

Joe Petrali, H-D's lone pro racer, set a national speed record aboard this Knucklehead-powered streamliner in 1937; however, this picture tells a story that's not quite accurate. First, the bodywork wasn't as slick or as stable as it appeared to be, so Petrali made the actual speed run, 136.183 miles per hour, on Daytona's beach with the bike bare. Next, the air cleaner on the left doesn't mean that the photo is flopped; it means there was a second carb for the Model E. And the generator has been replaced by a magneto. The tanks and the tail section are done up in Art Deco, just like the production bikes, because H-D wanted the public to get the impression that the record-setter was a lot more stock than it was. *Courtesy Harley-Davidson Archives*

He was a total professional. Born in San Francisco, Petrali began hanging around motorcycle shops at a very young age and assembled his first machine, an antique Indian single, when he was 13.

Petrali was such a good racer he got sponsorship from Indian, and when that firm dropped its team, Petrali was immediately hired by H-D. He was under contract, racing only, and kept his day job with Albert Crocker, an Indian dealer who later infuriated Harley-Davidson by building a 61-cubic-inch OHV motorcycle that was faster than Harley's equivalent. Petrali's allegiance was to racing, first and foremost. Back when he was racing Indians, he showed up at the track and discovered that his Indian had been lost in transit. As it turns out, a Harley guy had a bike that wouldn't run, so Petrali fixed it and rode to victory.

Petrali won hillclimbs on H-D's limited-edition, which was based on the D engine with overhead valves, and he won on the dirt and the board tracks with the 21- and 30-cubic-inch singles, known as "Peashooters" because of their exhaust notes.

In 1937 Petrali rode a modified Model E, the Knucklehead (see chapter 5), to a new national speed record of 136.183 miles per hour, at Daytona Beach. The photos show a streamlined tail section and fairing. In fact, the streamlining made the bike unstable so Petrali stripped the bodywork and muscled his way to the record.

Then came the new class, Class C, with big bikes and a different style, and Petrali didn't like them, or they didn't like him. So he went elsewhere, and when Howard Hughes defied the government and lifted the giant eight-engined Hercules (it wasn't made of spruce, and it wasn't named the Spruce Goose, except in the tabloids, but that's another legend for another time) into the air, the only other man in the airplane was the flight engineer, Joe Petrali.

A major factor in H-D's survival through the 1930s was police business. This 1934 VLD was first sold to a police department and fitted with a fire extinguisher as well as a siren and red light.

The OHV Model E was supposed to go into production for 1935, but it wasn't ready. The dealers needed something new, so H-D developed an 80-cubic-inch option for the sidevalve 74s, and the model carried over—witness this 1936 VLH—in case the Model E didn't make it.

professional classes had been called Class A and B, so the new class was called Class C, and the machine's owners, using production machines, would compete in it.

Because the most sporting production bikes were the 45-cubic-inch Harley Model R and the Indian Scout, 45 cubic inches was declared the eligible engine size, with sidevalves required. Some imports competed as well. One dealer in particular, Reggie Pink, sold Triumphs, Nortons, and other English bikes from his shop in the Bronx. He was an AMA member and a racer, so to be sure his customers could race, Class C was also open to 30-cubic-inch (better known as 500-cc) singles with overhead valves, which were the sporting English machines of the day. This was a bold move that worked. A generation of new stars, riders who wanted to race but couldn't buy a racing machine, appeared on the track, and brought their friends, and racing was revived, perhaps even improved.

CHAPTER 5

SPORT SAVES THE DAY

1936–1947

As the slogan goes, when the going got tough, Harley-Davidson got going. The tough part was, of course, the Great Depression, which hit the motorcycle business and the sport of racing especially hard. At that time a motorcycle was, for the most part, an option, an easily deferrable purchase, which most people did. H-D and Indian soldiered into the 1930s, however, keeping their corporate heads above water and depending on sales to police departments and other government agencies.

The H-D founders knew motorcycles, so early in these bad times, when they were cutting their own salaries and putting workers on part time, they authorized a new model, one that would be so new and exciting and sporting that the H-D fan would simply have to have one.

Discussions and preliminary planning began in 1931, but because the engineering department was

small and busy and there wasn't money to invest, the actual debut of the new machine, scheduled for 1935, was delayed until the 1936 model year.

The new bike, designated Model E and nicknamed Knucklehead, was worth the wait and the investment, evidenced by the fact that it would become the basis for Harleys in production 65 years later.

Not that the Model E was radical, because it wasn't. The engine was a 45-degree V-twin, with cylinders fore and aft and fork-and-blade connecting rods, just like the 1911 Harley V-twin. But the Knucklehead was an overhead valve (OHV) which gave the 61-cubic-inch engine more power than the H-D (or rival Indian) 74- or 80-cubic-inch sidevalve engines. (Harley had of course built OHV engines before, in single-cylinder street models and 45-cubic-inch hillclimbers, but until 1936, the extra cost hadn't been worth the return in sales.)

The E used a dual-stage oil pump, delivering oil from the tank to the engine and then scavenging the oil and sending it back to the tank—again, not radical; in fact, Indian had gone that route several years earlier. It was the modern way and a better way. The Model E also had a stronger and lower frame, and although the rear

The OHV 61 fills the frame's vee perfectly. The knuckles of the nickname are actually nuts for the rocker shafts atop the heads. One camshaft with four lobes was a departure from previous H-D practice. The device at right front, with the chromed cap, is the ignition timer.

The 1936 Knucklehead, formally the Model E, revived Harley-Davidson's fortunes and the motorcycle market, set the style for generations to come, and was the ancestor of the F-series engines of model year 2000.

wheel was solidly mounted, the clutch was operated by foot and the four-speed gearbox by hand.

This new model had what it took. It looked modern; it looked new; it looked right. And it sold. H-D's founders had been correct. Initial teething problems were quickly overcome. The Knucklehead was the fastest motor vehicle the buying public was likely to own or encounter, even capturing the national speed record in 1937.

The Motor Company then began playing from strength. The 45s (the R-series) were given recirculating oil systems, dry sump as we'd say now, and renamed the W-series. Because the 45s were the sport bikes, they were offered in a high-performance series, the W, WD, WDL, and WDLR. In 1941, Harley offered the WR— a stripped-for-racing version right off the showroom floor with no lights or brakes to unbolt. That model and the archrival Indian Sport Scout were the backbone of American racing for the next 10 years.

In terms of line and balance and distinctive looks, the Knucklehead was as good a motorcycle design as has ever been made.

229

By no accident whatsoever, the air-cooled Model E engine bore a strong resemblance to the air-cooled radial aircraft engines of the period. The container behind the engine is the oil tank, and the box behind that holds the tools.

The 45-cubic-inch middleweights followed the styling trends of the larger models but were renamed the W-series when they gained recirculating oil systems. (Hint for bike spotters: The middleweights from D through R and W and X have the final drive on the machine's right, while the larger models have the drive on the left.)

The 1939 WLDD, seen here at the vintage races in 1993, was the factory's high-performance model and came with special aluminum cylinder heads. It's rigged here for road racing and still has its brakes as well as a pad for riders when they are scooted back off the seat for lower wind resistance.

In 1937, the sidevalve twins were enlarged to 80 cubic inches and relettered U and UL, while the 61-cubic-inch E was joined by 74-cubic-inch versions, designated F and FL in 1941.

Then came the war. The United States, of course, entered World War II late in 1941, following the Pearl Harbor attack on December 7. But there were foresighted people in government and industry, so H-D, Indian, and the War Department had actually begun research for military motorcycles back in the mid-1930s.

H-D designed and built an experimental motorcycle patterned on the opposed-twin BMW, which was

This 1943 EL has the optional fat front wheel and tire, which was supposed to give a softer ride, and the round air cleaner fitted to the later Knucklehead engines, along with the instruments mounted on top of the fuel tanks and the fender trim. All these reappeared 50 years after this motorcycle was new.

previous spread
The army's motorcycle, the WLA, got raised suspension, extra clearance between fenders and tires so mud couldn't jam the wheels, a giant air cleaner, and a scabbard for a submachine gun. Although the motorcycle corps didn't see much combat, their cycles provided a valuable service as scouts and couriers.

By itself on a stand, the Knucklehead shows us where the name came from, with its polished nuts retaining the shafts for the rocker arms. The four-lobe camshaft is located where the pushrods intersect. The chromed cap to the right of the front pushrods is the ignition timer, which houses the points and condenser. The generator mounts at the front of the cases and is driven by a train of gears from the right-side flywheel. *Courtesy Harley-Davidson Archives*

This is a field meet and in some ways a parade as well. It is 1939, and the members of the Yonkers (New York) Motorcycle Club are dressed in semimilitary garb, which was popular before World War II put everybody in uniform; they are doing a precision drill at the Fishkill Gypsy Tour. In this era, clubs belonging to the AMA would often ride to a resort or park for a weekend of fun, games, and fellowship. *Courtesy Harley-Davidson Archives*

used effectively by the German Army, while Indian offered a cross-mount V-twin that their principal stockholder and CEO, Paul duPont, himself an inventor and engineer, had thought up.

The Allied forces used these motorcycles for scouting and courier duty, and H-D and Indian served the war effort by supplying tens of thousands of mildly modified sidevalve 45s, called, in Harley's case, the WLA—WL for the normal 45, A for the army version.

What Harley-Davidson had, in effect, was a series of niches. The W-series was for sport and competition; the E and F were the road burners and prestige models. Clark Gable had a Knucklehead, for instance, while the U and UL sidevalves hauled sidecars and did commercial

Pictured are the Milwaukee fairgrounds in 1947; the rider is Leo Anthony. You would suppose the machine to be a WR, the production racer. But no, not quite. That's a WR engine, all right, with a front end complete with an empty brake drum. But notice the double downtubes of the frame, the clutch lever on the left bar, and the shift lever in front of Anthony's boot. Ah ha! Now we know, 50 years later, that 5 years before the K and KR came out, the racing department was experimenting with stiffer frames, foot shift, and hand clutch. *Courtesy Harley-Davidson Archives*

DOT ROBINSON, RACER

Like most genuine heroines, Dot Robinson didn't set out to right wrongs or set the world straight. She just didn't see why gender should limit sport, so she didn't let it happen.

Many believe that women discovered motorcycles about the time they discovered the Feminist movement. Not so. As soon as the motorcycle appeared, there were women riding. They toured and raced and rode cross-country even back in the teens. There weren't that many female riders, but, nevertheless, women have always been part of the sport.

In Dot Robinson's case, her family's involvement in the motorcycle industry piqued her interest. Her family (the Gouldings) made sidecars for the big Harley twins. And through her motorcycle connections, Dot met and married Earl Robinson. He saw Dot at her family's shop and bought parts until she would date him.

It simply wouldn't have occurred to Dot Robinson that she shouldn't ride motorcycles, or that it was something ladies didn't do, so she did it. Dot and Earl became an impressive motorcycling team. This was in the 1930s, when only hard-core motorcyclists were riding and when the American highway system was just coming into being. The machines were markedly better than they'd been in pioneer days, so cross-country records were literally made to be broken, and

they were. In 1935 Dot and Earl set a New York–Los Angeles record in a Harley big twin fitted with a Goulding sidecar. Their time was 86 hours, 55 minutes, for the 3,000-plus miles.

Dot also rode enduros as a hobby, and legend has it that some people objected to girls getting all muddy, and there was talk of banning women. She heard the rumors, so, leaving Earl to mind the store, Dot rode cross-country on a mission. Face-to-face with each member of the AMA competition committee, she asked, "Are you going to try to stop me from competing?" And face-to-face, no man had the nerve to say anything beyond, "Gosh, no."

And that was that.

But the incident seems to have raised her consciousness, so in 1940 Dot and some other women created the Motor Maids, a feature of rallies and field meets for the next 20-plus years.

The Motor Maids had two main rules: One, membership was limited to women who rode their own, their husband's, or their father's motorcycles; and two, any member caught trailering her bike to an event was expelled from the club.

Dot rode her pink GLH well into the 1980s, always with good manners albeit, we suspect, we know what would have happened if she'd been challenged to a race. The Motor Maids are still a part of the sport, although now they're not quite so tough on the trailer queens.

This photo was taken in the 1940s, surely in the parking lot at H-D's Juneau Avenue headquarters. When this photo was first pried from the archives, the official word was that the bike was a road-racer made for Europe. Not so, mostly because the engine here looks to be a version of the DAH, a limited-production 750-cc (45-cubic-inch) OHV V-twin made for and used by the factory's hillclimbers in the late 1920s. Also, there was no 750 road-race class in Europe, and anyway, the Europeans had made importing motorcycles all but illegal. Not only that, the rider is dressed for the road, and the bike has a toolbox (the canister atop the front fender) and wears a rear stand. This machine was definitely made for highway use. Why did H-D develop this bike? Because early in the 1930s, before the Knucklehead was finalized, H-D's founders were thinking about a production OHV 45, like, oh, the Excelsior Super X, and this machine surely was an experiment in that direction, if not a prototype.
Courtesy Harley-Davidson Archives

work. And there was also the Servi-car, the three-wheeler towed by repair shops and used by police departments for parking meter enforcement.

H-D management has always had its corporate eyes open. For example, there were several prototype OHV 45s built before the founders decided that a true performance model had to be at least a 61. And the educated eye can scan the files and see hand clutches on racing bikes 10 years before they appeared on road machines. In keeping with this, even while busy with military work H-D knew the war would end, and that when it did, civilian demand would be stronger than ever.

However, they decided, first, to keep the existing models coming—no need to spend money on new stuff when the buyers will spring for the old, after all. At the same time, management wanted to enlarge the motorcycle market, which led in 1947 to the introduction of a single,

a 125-cc two-stroke based on a German (DKW) design, the rights to which H-D collected as part of its war effort.

Most of this plan worked out fine. The buyers were happy to collect the 45-, 74-, or 80-cubic-inch versions of the prewar machines, which gave H-D time to design and phase in the updates they knew were needed. At the same time, it's fair to say that this is when Harleys began to be seen as outmoded, which in many ways they were. Equally, we know the punchlines, that the upcoming new models would expand the factory's lineup, that the big bikes would create a market of their own, and beyond that, all the modern rivals would come to copy in the 1980s the looks that were outmoded in the 1940s.

CHAPTER 6

THE LITTLE ENGINES THAT DIDN'T

1947–1976

Harley-Davidson's single-cylinder models were, as Herbert Hoover said about Prohibition, "An experiment noble in purpose." The singles were, for the most part, good motorcycles, and so was the motivation behind the program. However, just as there is no thing stronger than an idea whose time has come, so is there no surer failure than the good idea whose timing is wrong.

The thinking was correct, surely. H-D's owners, along with the folks at Indian and those overseas, figured there would be a demand for motorcycles when World War II ended, and they hoped to attract new enthusiasts as well as the experienced crowd.

H-D engineers had no experience with little bikes. The beginner market had been dead for 15 years, after all. But at war's end Harley got the U.S. rights to use the German manufacturer DKW's design, saving a lot of time and expense.

A very different Harley-Davidson, the 125-cc two-stroke single introduced in 1947, was a direct copy of the prewar DKW. Note the girder forks, hand clutch, foot shift, and left-side kick-start.

The new model was a very basic motorcycle, as the DKW had been an inexpensive youth machine. Introduced in 1947 as a 1948 model and called either the M-125 or the S-125, the single displaced 125 cc produced around 3 brake horsepower, topped out at 55 miles per hour with the rider trailing his or her feet to reduce air drag, carried one person, weighed maybe 200 pounds, and had a wheelbase of 50 inches. Front suspension was a girder fork; the rear wheel was rigidly mounted in the frame, just like the big twins, but the 125 had a foot shift and hand clutch, a first for production Harleys.

H-D would later upgrade it, adding a telescopic fork and an engine enlarged to 165 cc; it was called the Hummer, and most of the little bikes are known by that name today.

One can't fault the factory for trying. H-D was willing to do what the market wanted—they offered the Pacer and the Scat; off-road singles and dual sport models; even several scooters, including one named Topper; and a couple of tiny bikes.

But still the machines didn't sell. Why? First, and the major factor, as it turned out, the public wasn't all that eager to ride motorcycles. And people who were interested often didn't like the old-boy atmosphere at the Harley store, while the old boys themselves, the dealers, weren't used to having young people in the place and didn't enjoy having to teach new buyers how to stay upright on the way home.

But while H-D struggled, it did not make the fatal mistake Indian did. In the late 1940s, Indian bet the farm on introducing the public to motorcycles. They advertised in the mass media, using movie stars such as Roy Rogers for spokespersons to sell their neat, small machines. These efforts failed, and it was clear at the time that Harley's *not* having tried to expand the market was why H-D was there and Indian was gone.

In the late 1950s, another company, Honda, had better luck with small machines. They advertised in the mass media as well, offering neat, small, and reliable (which the

The 1948 S-125, later nicknamed the Hummer, was small and basic but complete, even though they had to mount the horn outboard of the drive chain, behind the engine. And we'll see that tiny fuel tank again.

The Sprint had style. This is a 1964 in dual-sport trim with a high front fender, exhaust pipe, and even a case guard below the engine. It's Italian red, of course, and has a teardrop tank too shapely not to share.

The Sprint H was the sports version, but even so it came with a dual seat and full road gear. The box with the label contains the battery.

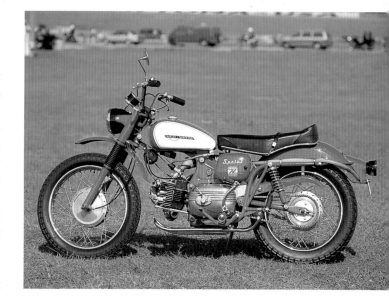

Indians weren't) motorcycles. Their slogan was "You Meet the Nicest People on a Honda," and this time the public went for it. The good idea had found its time.

H-D couldn't compete with Honda on a dollar-for-value basis, not with exchange rates and wages being what they were, nor could the company, still privately held, afford to build new designs. What they could do was buy a distressed Italian company, Aermacchi (which loosely translates into Airmachine) and import that maker's 250- and 350-cc four-stroke singles, calling them Harley-Davidson Sprint.

They were good little bikes, attractive and modern. The lovely teardrop tank, seen later on the touring

DICK O'BRIEN, RACING COACH

When we talk about a racing team, we often forget that racing is half the equation, and the other half is the team. And for a team, you need a coach.

No stick-and-ball squad ever had a coach more, well, more coachlike, than Dick O'Brien, who was head of the Harley racing team and department for many years. O'Brien began as a kid swapping work for parts, then as a racer of cars and motorcycles who realized that what he built went faster than he could ride it.

He joined The Motor Company as racing engineer in 1957. It was at this time that the sports bike, the Sportster, switched to overhead valves, while the racing bike, the KR, kept the sidevalves because H-D didn't have (or wouldn't spend) the money to make a road-legal 500-cc single to compete with the imports. H-D's flatheads remained competitive, thanks to being 750 cc, but it was really O'Brien's work that kept them equal. He was an engineer and worked out in the shop with the guys, honing and experimenting, and every year picked up a brake horsepower or two, until by 1968–1969, their last years, the KRs were producing 65 brake horsepower from 45 cubic inches.

But that is the mechanical side of the story.

The other side of the story reveals that O'Brien had a knack for getting the most out of those he worked with. He was a gruff bear with a deep, raspy voice that's just right for dressing down guilty parties. He cajoled and blustered and persuaded and almost always knew when to do which. He hired talent and fired talent when it got uppity. He played the press like a violin, handing out secrets when it served the team's interest, clamming up when it didn't. He bolstered morale when it sagged and played tuners and riders against each other when rivalry made the rivals work harder.

Harley-Davidson has long had mandatory retirement, but nobody who saw "O.B." in action ever doubted that he stayed on the job well past the limit, because there wasn't anybody in H-D's head office brave enough to tell him to leave before he was ready, which he was in 1985.

Sportsters and early Superglides, came from the sporting version of the Sprint and was too good to not use over and over. But, again, the public didn't go for them. The Sprints came in touring, sporting, dirt, or racing form. They were squeezed into streamliners and set records at Bonneville. They were the basis for the factory's short-track and 250-class road-racing efforts, and the public could buy kits to build or convert racing machines for privateer efforts.

Still they didn't sell. It's true, the little Italian machines needed more care and understanding than the big twins did, and the young crowd buying small singles was more apt to abuse and neglect them than the old guys were, but even so, part of the problem was that the Sprints weren't native Harley-Davidsons, so to speak, and the other part of the problem was that in sheer technical terms they weren't up to Japanese standards or even up to date.

That came next. Two-stroke engines had taken over in off-road, as in enduros and motocross, so Harley-Davidson switched too and had Aermacchi

Sprints became a mainstay of amateur competition and were even used in professional short-track events. This is the 350-cc model, an ERS, with the production engine fitted to a lightweight frame, available through the factory.

make a line of two-stroke singles, in dual sport (road legal), enduro, and motocross forms. The factory sponsored a full team in motocross and even innovated, making rear suspensions that looked like the sliders and stanchion tubes that were used for the by-then-worldwide telescopic forks in front.

By the 1970s, Harley-Davidson was in trouble. H-D had limited resources. There'd been the expansion into small motorcycles and scooters and golf carts, which weren't selling, and there were the traditional twins, the Sportsters, Superglide, and FLHs, which were selling.

In short, Harley-Davidson went back out of the small motorcycle market. Sold them all, on the floor and off, even threw in a trailer if you'd buy the bike.

The sad part is obvious, in that the little Harleys were good motorcycles and the effort failed through no fault of their own.

The unfair part is that the critics have long yammered about how Harley-Davidson has kept on cranking out those air-cooled, pushrod-operated overhead-valve (OHV) twins when the world has gone elsewhere, while in fact and as this record shows, H-D has made a valiant effort to meet the public's demands: it's the fickle public that's the culprit here.

The good side to the story is that despite failing to make a dent in the small motorcycle market, H-D weathered the storms and remains financially strong. It may even be safe to bet that we'll see the Harley range broaden in the near future, and that the single will return.

CHAPTER 7

THE BIG
TWIN ERA

1948 - 1980

Radical tradition, when applied to Harley-Davidson, isn't the contradiction it would be elsewhere. In 1948, having satisfied the demand for just about anything with an engine, Harley-Davidson made a major change to big twins.

The E and F models, with 61- and 74-cubic–inch engines, respectively, got new cylinder heads. They were made of aluminum, and they used hydraulic valve lifters—this at a time when Detroit still relied on iron components. The new heads used a rocker cover that looked (if you used your imagination) like a cake pan, leading the fans to call the new models Panheads.

Just as soon as the new top end proved itself, the rest of the motorcycle was brought up to date, step by step. (H-D's leaders knew they could offer the old stuff when the market allowed, and knew to improve when improvement was demanded.)

Thirty years after the Knucklehead, the Panhead was replaced by this top end, known as the Shovelhead. The three engines were different in detail but shared a basic structure and many components.

In 1949 the leading-link forks, which dated back to 1907, were replaced with telescopic front suspension. The model designation remained F or FL, but the factory coined the name Hydra Glide. In 1958 the rigidly mounted rear wheel was given suspension: conventional shock absorbers and swingarm, and the still-FL was named the Duo Glide. In between, as it were, hand clutch and foot shift became an option for the big twins, beginning in 1952, although for several model years the old hand shift and foot clutch were listed as standard and the newly swapped controls were supposedly an option, even though all but the hard-core few went with the new (and better) way.

Thus, the Knucklehead and early Panhead were built in 74- and 61-cubic-inch form, while the factory first phased out the sidevalve big twins and then the 61 overhead-valve (OHV) Panhead. The 61 had been a low-stress model and was replaced by a mild version of the FL. At the same time, the factory offered a 74 with polished intake ports and camshaft timing, and it claimed a 10 percent boost in power. Its designation was FLH, the H representing an improvement, as seen with the J and JH (the H does not stand for Highway or Hot).

Along with the smaller models detailed elsewhere, Harley-Davidson began experimenting with diversification and became interested in plastics and fiberglass. This led in turn to the use of the new materials for saddlebags.

The FL and FLH were offered with plastic or fiberglass saddlebags, along with larger fuel tanks and windshields.

Perhaps the major leap into modern times came in 1965, when the Panhead, named the Duo Glide after rear suspension was offered in 1958, got electric start and became the Electra Glide. This conquered a

Why it's called the Panhead is obvious; less obvious is that this 1948 FL still has the springer forks, rigid rear wheel, and hand shift inherited from the Knucklehead.

Where the Hydra Glide gets its name is equally obvious. Telescopic forks were new for this 1949 Panhead, along with a right-side chromed hub cover to mimic the front brake on the left.

Rear suspension brought the name Duo Glide. This 1959 FLH also has a hand clutch and foot shift—the rocker above the left-side floorboard. And that spring-thing above the rocker? That's a helper spring for the clutch, which was designed for foot power. The helper's imaginative nickname is Mousetrap.

major obstacle (even though many Harley folks had looked on the electric leg unfavorably since 1914, when Indian offered electric start only to withdraw the option because the batteries of 1914 weren't up to the job). While kick-starting a big motorcycle is wonderfully satisfying when it works, it's shamefully frustrating when the engine doesn't respond. Not only

that, the Japanese had made electric start standard and cheap and effective, making the other manufacturers appear behind the times.

As soon as the electric start worked, the factory took another major step, for 1966, with new cylinder heads—the Shovelhead. It was so called because the rocker boxes look, if you use your imagination, like

The improved Panhead engine justified electric starting, which arrived in 1965 with the Electra Glide. The kick-start is still there (as the early electric starters did give trouble), while the massive battery literally displaced the toolbox.

the business end of a coal shovel. The new heads used improved flow and higher compression and raised the power again, while being cleaner and quieter in operation than the Panhead had been. As you can see by the following numbers, the added power wasn't so much noticed as it was needed.

According to historian Jerry Hatfield, the early 1940s FL with springer forks weighed 550 pounds, presumably dry but fully equipped. The 1964 FL, weighed by *Cycle World* with half a load of fuel, topped out at 690 pounds, while the electric starter and bigger battery added at least 75 pounds. And *Cycle World*'s test 1967 FLH weighed in at 783 pounds. Thus, the 60-brake-horsepower FLH option wasn't too much power, not compared with a 515-pound Panhead rated at 48 brake horsepower.

The big Harley was no longer the performance king. Instead, quoting from the factory's brochure for the optional package of saddlebags, top box, and fairing, the FLH was King of the Highway, defining if not inventing the touring motorcycle.

Fashion, of course, demands change, so when some Harley riders began adding bags, boxes, case guards, fairings, lights, fringe, and so forth, other Harley riders began taking things off.

At first they mimicked the TT racers, adding raised suspension and exhaust and small tanks to their big twins; then they went beyond function, with high pipes, extended forks, and no front brake or fender. The creations were called choppers, and they mostly were for show.

But then Willie G. Davidson, who, like his grandfather's partner, had gone off to get an engineering degree and came back to the family firm, saw an opportunity. The design staff took an FL frame and engine, installed the lighter XL front suspension and light, and

The King of the Highway package was touring equipment, as seen on this 1966 FLH wearing a windshield and fiberglass boxes on the rear fender. This example has front and rear case guards, dual exhausts, and every chromed cover known to the accessory division.

Here's a Harley that never was. When the English and Japanese triples and fours eclipsed the Sportster as a performance bike, the engineers at Juneau Avenue considered answering in kind producing this mock-up of an overhead cam, 750-cc V-twin with a 50-degree included angle. It has Sportster bars, lights, and fenders, an XR-750 fuel tank, and an XR-based frame. But budget constraints overruled the project, so the larger (and cheaper to build) XL-1000 carried on. This machine went directly from the drawing board to the history book.

Courtesy Harley-Davidson Archives

THE AMF ERA

By the end of the 1960s, Harley-Davidson's founders had died and the company had gone public but didn't have the working capital to take advantage of the motorcycling boom caused by the arrival of Honda and others. So, early in 1969, Harley-Davidson was acquired by American Machine and Foundry, better known as AMF, a conglomerate working on the notion that leisure industries were a good place to be and on the notion that motorcycles are a leisure industry.

By unhappy chance, the takeover came at the same time as a boom in sport and off-road motorcycles and at a time of change and disquiet across the cultural span.

H-D wasn't prepared for motocross, the Honda 750, the Triumph triple, or the Kawasaki 900. The federal government had begun imposing rules, such as requiring that all gearshifts had to be on the right with neutral between first and second, not to mention emissions regulations. And all of this came at a time when H-D was embroiled in labor troubles, resulting in serious problems for The Motor Company.

Some thought AMF had bought H-D so they could lose money doing a poor job making inferior motorcycles. It's true that AMF management didn't understand motorcycling and made some poor decisions. Most likely H-D survived only because of a loyal dealer and owner network. But because AMF did spend lots of money on the plant (versus spending it on the product or the people), the AMF ownership ultimately kept H-D in business and set the stage for success down the road.

You can't have a silver lining unless you begin with a cloud.

The Superglide made its first appearance in 1971. It created a lot of news and attention because the Superglide didn't look like anything H-D had ever produced.

Outrageous, eh? The original Wide Glide was totally chopper as you can tell by the flared rear fender, raked forks, high bars, and flamed tank. And this was the last time step-start was offered on a production H-D. *Courtesy Harley-Davidson Archives*

added a fiberglass seat and rear fender, which was first seen as a seldom-ordered option for the Sportster.

The experiment was shown in public in the late 1960s, with the factory's involvement not mentioned. The reaction was favorable, and in 1971, the FX, named for the F-series engine and X-series parts, was introduced as the Superglide. It was a big hit, once the press and the public got used to the idea of a production chopper. And later, when the big tanks were swapped for the lovely teardrop tank from the Sprint and when electric start was standard, the Superglide sold.

Partly through intuition and partly by taking the right notes, the people in charge of H-D had set the styles for what was to come.

HIGH-PERFORMANCE RETURNS

1 9 5 2 – 1 9 8 5

While Harley-Davidson's post–World War II plan was to continue production on the big bikes and make radical moves with the lightweight models, they ended up developing a line of sporting middleweights. H-D was pushed in this direction by a buying public that was enamored with British bikes, especially the 500-cc and 650-cc twins.

H-D's first move in 1952 was to replace the W-series (the sidevalve 45s) with a new model line that was more different than it looked.

The series name was K. The new bikes still had a 45-degree V-twin engine with valves on the side of the bore, and its 45 cubic inches translated into 750 cc. But the K differed in that it used unit construction, with the transmission a cluster of gears on shafts tucked into a cavity in the rear of the engine cases,

The profile of the K engine, with its narrow-vee center carb and arc of four one-lobe camshafts below the valves, is still an H-D trademark 50 years later. The shift lever was on the right, like the British rivals and unlike the bigger Harleys.

instead of having an actual gearbox bolted to the back of the engine.

And the K had telescopic forks and a swingarm rear suspension, with four speeds forward, foot shift, and hand clutch, fully as modern as anything from England, Italy, or Germany.

Included in the K-series was the basic, street-going Model K, the mildly souped-up KK, and the race-only KR, a highly tuned engine in a racing-spec frame; both the KK and KR were much more different from the road version than they looked, plus you could buy a swingarm and shock absorbers to bolt onto the KR frame and add brakes, a big fuel tank, and later a streamline fairing to make a KRTT. There was also a desert racer, basically a KR engine in a K frame, called the KRM.

While the K had looks and specifications, it lacked power. So in 1954 the engine was given a longer stroke, increasing displacement to 883 cc, and it was relettered the KH. H-D also made a tuned version, the rare KHK, and the even more rare KHR and KHRTT, the purposes of which can be guessed by the letters.

The 1952 Model K, with telescopic forks, rear swingarm, and unit construction engine and transmission, was about as all-new as any Harley since the WJ Sport of 1919.

The KR and KRTT were a match for the imports at the races but sales were lackluster at best, so in 1957 H-D took the last step to conventional wisdom, introduced an overhead-valve (OHV) engine for the sporting crowd, and invented the mass-produced Superbike. The name was Sportster, surely as good a name for a motorcycle as has ever been thought up, equal to, oh, Thunderbird or Black Lightning.

The designation was XL. Odd, in a Harley-Davidson sense, because the X was a repeat: a World War II–era machine done for the military but never produced as a civilian bike was designated XA, with the A for Army. Plus, H-D had until then used one letter, as in J, E, or W, for the basic model. The in-house guess has always been that there was a plain X at one

The seldom-seen KHK was a K with a larger and more highly tuned engine. It sold by the handful, perhaps because the lack of visible differences subtracted from the brag potential.

The KR was all racer, with highly modified internals behind the K profile and with a special frame that could mount either a rigid section for dirt-track racing, as seen here, or a swingarm with shocks for TT or road races. And yes, the fuel tank came from the little 125-cc Hummer.

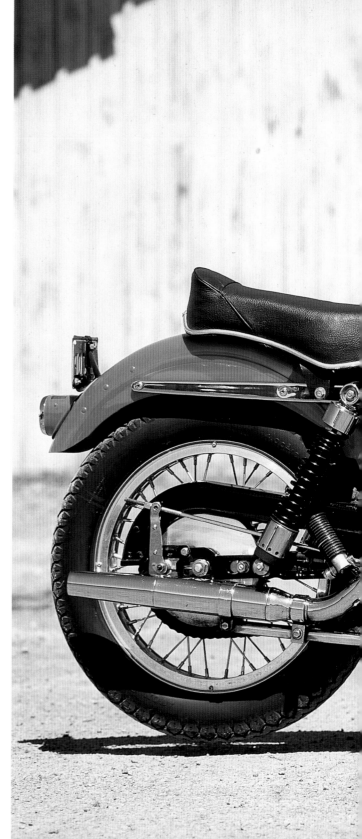

The first XL, the 1957 Sportster, mimicked the look of the K-series, except that the OHV engine was a lot more different from the K or KH than it looked. And the XL's big fuel tank and headlight nacelle made it a little brother to the FL series.

time, but the tuned version, as in JD or FL, worked so well the X was never produced. That's a guess.

More important here, most of the XL was just like the KH, as in suspension, unit construction, and so forth. The XL engine displaced 883 cc, again like the KH, but the XL had overhead valves, a higher compression ratio, bigger bore and shorter stroke, all of which meant more power and performance.

The Sportster was an instant success—mostly because the factory listened to the market. The first XL was almost a junior FLH, but when the dealers asked for speed and sport, the factory offered the XLC, a stripped XL for desert racing in California, and the XLR, a mix of XL and KR parts, and they topped the mix with the XLCH, an instant classic with a tuned engine, a "peanut" fuel tank from the KR (which took it from the little Hummer), low, dual exhausts, low bars, and a solo seat.

There is a lot of history captured here, as the XLCH had a tuned XL engine fitted with two single exhaust pipes, the magneto ignition, and the ex-Hummer fuel tank used first by the KR. This was also the origin of the hamcan air cleaner and the little eyebrow mount for the headlight, both still in production.

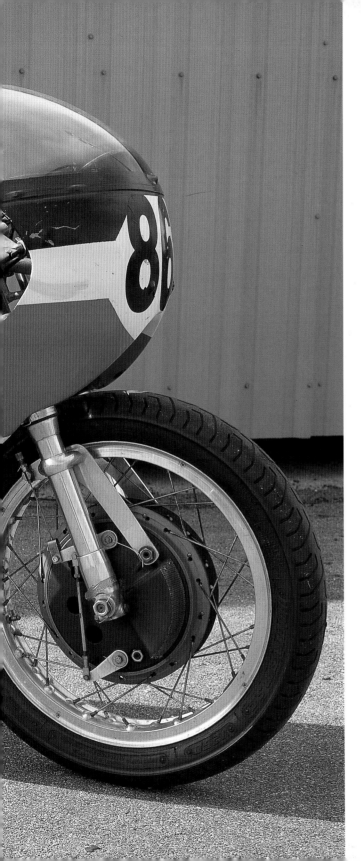

This is a factory publicity shot, posed to introduce the XLCH in 1959. The studio has gone to lots of trouble propping the bike in an attack mode, but nobody bothered to have the guy change into riding gear rather than slacks and shoes. Never mind, what is most significant now is that this is the first use of that eyebrow headlight mount and small light, and of the small peanut fuel tank the XLCH got from the KR, which in turn borrowed it from the Hummer. *Courtesy Harley-Davidson Archives*

The XLCH was the original mass-produced Superbike, more than a match for the imports. One reason H-D went to using 883 cc on the label rather than 54 cubic inches was because the imports were 650s and then 750s. As we all know, bigger is better.

In 1968, there was a divergence in the series. The XLH was offered with electric start, while the XLCH still had kick-start only. And then the competition came out with triples and fours and even bigger twins, which meant that the Sportster no longer ruled the street.

The factory countered with a larger 1,000-cc version, which had options such as a larger fuel tank, a thicker seat, and a fiberglass seat and rear fender (nicknamed boattail). H-D even tried for a vaguely racer

In its final form, the 1968–69 Lowboy seen here, the KR-TT was highly specialized and still effective, in that it won the Daytona 200 both years, against much newer rivals. The KR-TT had its own frame, Italian brakes and front suspension, full bodywork developed in the wind tunnel, and a ferociously tuned version of that sidevalve K engine. The 1968 team bikes were the first to use the Team Harley orange and black paint.

look called the XLCR, CR standing for Café Racer, an English fad at one time. The XLCR didn't sell, which of course made it instantly collectible.

The XL line was also the basis for a lot of competition involvement, as the drag racers discovered it was easier to make the XL engine bigger than it was to keep the FL engine together. The second actual XL model was the XLR, a stripped-and-souped mixture of the XL and KR used for national TTs, where for some obscure reason there was still an Open class. By the late 1960s, however, the XL proper lost its performance mantle to the two-strokes, triples, and fours and became more practical and useful at the same time with lots of options, including big tanks and windshields.

The Sportster was adapted to the changing times, which were changing at great speed. In 1981, a group of H-D managers, members of the founding families, and so execs brought in by AMF put up all the money they had or could borrow and bought The Motor Company from the corporation.

The slogan was "The Eagle Flies Alone." The fact was, the eagle was burdened by the need to service a tremendous debt. As one way to increase sales and get

continued on page 79

CALVIN RAYBORN AND THE KR

Realists, or perhaps the cynics, like to say there's no such thing as luck in racing, and it's true, the winner is most often the person who's stayed up latest and worked the hardest.

Plus, there is talent—and when there's mention of talent, you have to include Calvin Rayborn.

He was a shagger, zooming around San Diego on whatever motorcycle he could find, dropping off blueprints and legal papers. Then he went to the races and came to the attention of Len Andres, the San Diego H-D dealer who'd tuned son Brad to the national title in 1955.

Andres began building bikes for Rayborn, and Rayborn turned out to be a natural talent, arguably the best of his era. In 1968, after the KRTT wore orange and black for the first time, and the factory team filled Daytona's first two rows, Rayborn not only won the 200, he lapped the field.

In 1969, the two-strokes were there, and the KRTTs were slower than they'd been the previous year. Yamahas got the pole and 7 of the first 10 places, while the Harleys were 10 miles per hour off the pace. And then, on race day, it rained. The 200 was postponed for a week, so team guru Dick O'Brien had time to find out why the KRs had slowed down, and it turned out to be the new dual carbs, which were fixed.

When the racing finally resumed, the fastest Yamaha's ignition fell off, the fastest Suzuki threw its rider off—and Cal Rayborn won again, riding a KRTT that was, to quote *Cycle*, "definitely not the fastest thing around."

It was the KR's last hurrah, and finest hour, and best of luck.

The XLCH Café Racer was a good try that didn't work. It was a mix of a stock XL-1000 engine, an improved frame derived from the XR-750, some XR styling hints, a bikini fairing, and black paint. The public wasn't interested in blending dirt track with European profiler, and the XLCR didn't sell.

The XR-750 began winning dirt track races in 1972, and the team guys say they'll win with XRs in 2000. An XR is a specialized, highly evolved racer, but this one, which was raced by pro contender Jason Fletcher, still displays that K-model profile and the ex-Hummer, now peanut, fuel tank.

XR-750, TIMELESS RACING MACHINE

Back in 1934, when the factories and the dealers and the AMA set out to save racing, they agreed on the equivalency formula, 750-cc sidevalve versus 500-cc OHV. It worked well for 35 years, but by 1969 the imports weren't selling many 500-cc models and Harley's venerable KR was the only sidevalve left. The AMA, with heavy pressure from the importers, came up with new rules, allowing any 750-cc engine produced in quantity and sold to the public.

H-D's overnight answer, when the team was short of money and time, was a destroked version of the XLR, named the XR-750 and based on the iron-top XL engine. The iron XRs were lovely to look at, but their engines blew up early and often.

In 1972, having taken the time, been given the money, and learned the lesson, the race team built the alloy XR-750, with better material, shorter stroke, bigger bore, more power, and longer life.

The XR-750 was the machine for dirt track—miles, half-miles, and TT, while the XRTT, a different frame with the same two-carb engine and an efficient fairing (based on the late KRTT glass) ran the road courses.

The four-stroke twin couldn't compete on pavement with the fours or the two-strokes, however, so by 1975 H-D was out of road racing. But the narrow-angle V-twin is still the best on dirt, and at the turn of the century, Harley's XR-750, in all the basics just as it was in 1972, is still the best in the class.

While most XR-750s can be found turning left and spitting roost on the flat tracks of America, a select few have been converted for street use. Who is up for feet-up broadslides onto Main Street?

The XR-1000 combined elements of the XR-750—the two-carb heads and dual exhausts—and the peanut fuel tank and the XLX-style solo seat. The price was high, the reliability low, and the sales dismal.

The Evolution Sportster has been a top seller since its 1986 introduction, and it's now offered as a sport, a custom, or even a racer.

Continued from page 74
some ink, in 1983 H-D introduced the XLX, a barebones, loss-leader Sportster with a solo seat, black-only paint, low bars, no extras, and a sticker price of $3,995. The bikes sold as fast as they could be made, while the campaign that came with the model helped turn the corner, as Harleys became, after some years of disfavor, the bike to buy.

With two such steps forward, there had to be one step back. And there was. Also for 1983, the factory tried to cash in on the success of the race-winning XR-750 and mixed that machine's two-carb heads, alloy top end, and high dual exhaust pipes with the XLX trim and peanut tank.

The model name was XR-1000. It didn't offer all that much performance and the sticker price was $7,000, so sales were dismal. Worse, the few who did buy discovered the engine was fragile, so much so that the factory had a new run of engine cases done at the foundry. Perhaps worst, the XR-1000 didn't look all that different, which meant H-D was sort of selling a Ferrari in a Fiat suit.

But wait, there are two bright spots here. One, because the public wasn't sold, the collectors swept in and kept the prices up. Two, while the XLX sold and won new buyers for Harley, it was a loss leader, but because the price for the XR-1000 was so high, sources in the factory say each one sold at profit.

So even when it lost, the Lone Eagle won.

CHAPTER 9

INDEPENDENCE AND EVOLUTION

1980 – 1997

While the grudge many Harley lovers have against the American Machine and Foundry has died extremely hard, AMF did at least one favorable thing during its ownership—they authorized the engineering and investment of the FLT.

The timing was nearly perfect. In 1980, Harley-Davidson unveiled the new FLT model. It had the F-series engine, enlarged to 80 cubic inches but in a new frame and with a frame-mounted fairing instead of the batwing barmount fairing used by the now-classic FLH. More important, the FLT engine and transmission were isolated from the riders by shock-absorbent mounts (the mounts are often called rubber, but strictly speaking, they are made of a different material).

The FLT was big—and it worked, in essence redefining the touring motorcycle and putting H-D in the news as well as selling.

The V2 (Evolution) engine was nearly new, but its ancestry can easily be confirmed by comparing it with the Knucklehead portrait in chapter 5. *Courtesy Harley-Davidson Archives*

Soon after, some members of the Davidson family, some old-line H-D guys, and some executives who'd come to H-D from AMF, bought H-D from AMF, putting up all the money they had and mortgaging their futures to make up the difference. This was a win-win move. AMF wanted to get out of the leisure business, and Harley's new owners thought the corporate atmosphere soaked up too much time and energy.

With the new ownership in place, H-D continued to innovate. And, while the AMF managers hadn't been bikers, gearheads, or party animals, they'd authorized the engineering and investment for, first, the FLT.

In 1981, H-D introduced the FXR. It had the same isolation-mount principle as the FLT, but in another new, much lighter frame. The FXR came in sport and touring versions, the former generally acclaimed as the best Harley ever made, the latter an excellent bike but too conventional. Import riders didn't want a Harley; Harley buyers didn't want to look like the imports.

The original plan was that the FXR would replace the original FX line and be called the Superglide II. This didn't happen. Instead, while developing improvements such as a five-speed transmission for the big twins and a

The FXB Sturgis was named for the South Dakota rally, and the black-with-polished-alloy theme was radical. But the real difference was the final drive, with a notched belt and pulleys replacing the chain for the first time in nearly 50 years.

Next came the Evolution, the V2 engine, seen here in a custom-painted 1985 FXR. The V2 engine was traditional in broad specs and in outline, but it was virtually trouble-free, while the FXR handled like a sports bike and looked as new as it was.

The Heritage Softail defines nostalgia. Not only does this 1991 example look as if it has the rigid rear wheel of its ancestors, the owner has added a toolbox and a horn with a bell, and once again, you can get just about any paint scheme you can imagine.

belt final drive for the Harley twins, the engineers had been working on something even bigger—a new engine. Well, it was new in the sense that almost all of the parts were new, as well as improved, but at the same time the V2 engine, quickly nicknamed "Blockhead" by *Cycle World,* was an 80-cubic-inch, 45-degree, air-cooled, two-valve, four-stroke, single-camshaft engine. In other words, it had generally the same specs as the Shovelhead, the Panhead, and the Knucklehead.

The Blockhead, now generally known as the Evo, was phased into the big twin line, phased because meanwhile, Harley's guys had been to a show and seen an outsider's notion of building a rear suspension; it was tucked beneath the frame rails and made the bike look

CHARLEY THOMPSON, THE PERFECT PRESIDENT

There are no blueprints for creating top executives, but if there were, Charley Thompson would have been the perfect pattern for H-D—except perhaps that Thompson had a misspent childhood and didn't ride a motorcycle until he was in his thirties.

When he did take that first fateful ride, he was a high-school teacher and football coach, but he liked motorcycling so much he became a Harley dealer. He was so good at that, he became H-D's national sales manager. And he was so good at that, he became H-D's president when H-D was reclaimed from AMF.

In his dealership days, Thompson used intuition and his own experience to formulate a basic piece of wisdom: The most important thing a dealer can offer is something for the customers to do on their bikes. Thus, as president he instituted the quality control program, giving the workers the chance to do good work and to take pride in their work, leading in turn to a product the customers could trust and take pride in.

That done, in 1982 he climbed aboard a stock FLT with a sealed engine so there'd be no tricks and rode it, flawlessly, from the Pacific Coast to Daytona Beach. He died in 1988, and those who knew Charley still miss him.

This 1992 Ultra Classic FLT is called a dresser because it has extra lights along with a sound system and every chrome extra in the catalog.

like the old rigid-rear motorcycles. H-D licensed the idea, and it became, for the 1984 model year, the Softail. (For the record, the in-crowd bikers called the old-time, rigid-rear bikes Hardtails.)

This was a tremendously successful move. The original Superglides evolved into a model line, with different paint, larger (21-inch instead of 19-inch) front wheels, and a belt drive. The Softails were in 1984 what the Superglide had been in 1971, the hot ticket. And just as the Superglide demanded dues in the form of kick-start, so did the Softail scorn the isolation mounts of the FLT and FXR. The Evo engine bolted directly to the FXST's frame because, in the spirit of William Harley, real motorcycles vibrate and real motorcyclists want it that way!

And William Harley, the man who designed the leading-link forks of 1907, had his design brought back in 1988 on the Softail—leading-link forks. While markedly improved and refined, the Springer was essentially the same concept that first appeared decades earlier.

The bar-mount fairing returned on the FLHT because some buyers didn't like the frame-mount fairing of the FLT. As these three bikes demonstrate, however, it's the same frame, full touring rig, and V2 engine on either model.

273

H-D's newest model line is the Dyna Glide, which replaced the FXR. This is a 1995 FXD. The framework bolted to the fender brace behind the rear shock is a mount for luggage, meaning this is an FXD Convertible, with touring gear that can be mounted or removed in minutes.

The Road King, seen here in 1996 model trim, was an FLT minus extras including fairing, top box, and sound system, saving weight and money.

The Heritage Springer was new for 1997 and used the big front wheel and tire with the revived leading-link forks, making this model a combination of two popular trends. The blue-dot turn signal lenses, backrest, and duffel bag are extras.

The tradition of evolution, making one change and seeing how it works, then making another change, had become The Motor Company's motto.

For 1986 the Sportster XLX kept the designation but got a new engine, the Evolution XL, with the same bore, stroke, and displacement (883 cc) as the original 1957 XL. But the new engine shared only a few parts with the original; it was all alloy instead of having cast-iron heads and barrels. Next, the 883 grew into an 1,100 and then a 1,200; bikes with the optional dual seats and big tanks became models of their own, and there was even the Hugger, a lowered XLH that was intended for women, not that H-D ever admitted this.

The Evolution era was a revolution, in the sense that the new mechanical bits were so much better than what they replaced. They attracted buyers who wouldn't have gone inside an old-time Harley store. Some dealers won't even work on anything made before 1984.

More important in this era was that H-D went public, sold stock, and got out of hock, becoming a financial fairy tale praised round the world. Harley-Davidson became a business legend not because of technical advances, but because H-D could, first, read the public pulse and second, fill a lot of niches with not a lot of parts. It was kind of like having Ford, Ferrari, and Honda under one roof.

The Sportster became the best-selling motorcycle model in the United States—not the best big bike, but the best-seller period. The FLT and FLHT (the one with the batwing fairing) were the class of the touring class. And the XR-750 ruled the national championship.

Everyone who was someone had a Harley. Even celebrities were shown in the tabloids careening around on Softail Heritages, wearing I-Got-Attitude T-shirts.

All this from what amounted to variations on two engines and four or so frames, mixed, matched, juggled, swapped, and disguised.

275

CHAPTER 10

NEW AND IMPROVED

1994–2000

Harley-Davidson swept into the 1990s on a roll, selling all the motorcycles they could make and enlarging the factories so they could make more. Much of this success can be attributed to H-D's attention to details that were important to buyers. During the early and middle part of the decade, the focus was on fine-tuning. The changing of a few cosmetic details allowed H-D to offer many different models without too much hassle.

One example of this can be seen with the FLHT. The buying public liked the FLHT with the batwing fairing better than the original rubber-mount FLT, so the FLT was dropped from the line at the end of 1996, and then returned to production in 1998 with a shorter screen and was called the Road Glide. The FLT's basic frame and engine, meanwhile, had been offered with a windshield and called the sport option, but when it became popular in 1994—it was the lightest and, therefore, the most nimble of the T-series—it

The new Twin-Cam 88 motor is a modern interpretation of an early 20th century design.

was renamed the Road King. And, of course, there was the Electra Glide. You really do need a catalog to keep track of the players.

Another attempt on H-D's part to appeal to the buyers involved the FXR-series. This series had been phased out in favor of the Dyna Glides, to the dismay of the more sports-oriented Harley crowd. And then, in 1998, the FXR returned. Briefly. There were 900 FXR2s and 900 FXR3s made (and snapped up.) The factory reproduced the frames, fitted V2 engines, and did half the run, the R2, with a 21-inch front wheel and slotted rear wheel, and the other half, the R3, with 19-inch front and a flamed fuel tank.

Factory spokespersons said they didn't discover 1,800 leftover FXR frames in a barn; they instead wanted to test H-D's ability to produce special runs of special models, so that's what they did. They also claimed to have no plans to build any more FXRs.

In addition to all the fine-tuning, in 1998 Harley-Davidson introduced another engine, a bigger twin, and like its predecessors, it was as much new as it was improved. Its name is the Twin Cam 88. Note that the big twin went from E to F when it grew from 61 to 74

The Night Train was a 1999 Softail with black crackle paint, forward controls—that's the rear brake lever way up there in front of the exhaust pipe—and the V2 single-cam engine.

cubic inches but kept the F designation when it became the 80 and then the 88.

The Twin Cam 88 has, no surprise, two camshafts, one for each cylinder, with a straighter and less variable path from camshaft lobe to rocker arm. And the engine displaces 88 cubic inches, thanks to a shorter stroke and much larger bore, but it's still a 45-degree V-twin, is air-cooled, and has its cylinders directly aligned fore and aft.

So, although the Twin Cam shares only 18 parts with the V2, it's still another descendant of the 1936 Model E. And while the five-speed gearbox is techni-cally a separate component, the mounting of engine to primary to gearbox is so rigid as to make the Twin Cam a unit design in everything except name.

Starting in 1998, the Twin Cam engine was phased into production, using fuel injection for the topline FL touring models and a carburetor for the Dyna fitted with the new powerplant.

The Evo big twin remained in production for two more model years, in the Softails; the factory said this was because Softail buyers liked the traditional shakes and rattles.

continued on page 94

The 1999 Road King, seen here with windshield detached, came with the twin-cam 88 engine; the quick way to spot the new engine is the oval air cleaner.

SPORTSTERS FOREVER

Somehow, until now, there's been no mention of the Harley-Davidson official motto: If It Ain't Broke, Don't Fix It.

The motto's evidence is the Sportster, still the XL-series, still 883 or 1,200 cc, still four one-lobe cams, still with air cooling. Just about every part had been changed since its 1957 introduction, but the specs are the same, and sales are higher than ever for its several versions—the Sport, the Custom, and the lowered Hugger. There is even an AMA-series for XLs stripped and raced on dirt tracks and road courses, just like the original Class C races of 1938.

The Sportster is still the Sportster, which must rank it right alongside the Ford Model T and VW's original Beetle in terms of living long and prospering.

ERIC BUELL, ENTREPRENEUR

In 1983, Eric Buell, an engineer and racer, left Harley-Davidson and formed his own motorcycle company. Buell had the rights to a racing-only 750-cc two-stroke and went into business just in time for the 750 race-engine class to be abandoned. So he bought up Harley's supply of XR-1000 engines, in surplus at the home plant, and began building race and semirace machines with radical, lightweight frames, full streamlining, and Harley power.

What entrepreneurs do best is move fast and take chances. Buell did both, and each time he brought out another model it was better and more useful and sold in larger numbers. There were teething problems, but Buell buyers, like Harley owners in the past, so liked the good days that they ignored the bad days, until Buell had the money and expertise to produce usable sports bikes, different and fast, using modified XL engines.

Harley-Davidson noticed this. And the managers knew they had a problem of their own. A large share of the H-D market was based on nostalgia and fad—being the first guy on the block to have a new Harley that looked like an old Harley.

So in 1997, Harley-Davidson bought majority control of Buell, giving him the capital and technical backing needed to produce inventive, daring, and legal motorcycles.

Early Buells were race-oriented, fully enclosed, and about as graceful as this RR-1000, powered by the XR-1000 engine, looks. They didn't win races, and they didn't sell.

Current Buells, for instance this 1999 X1 Lightning, are lighter, faster, more agile, and do win races. Power comes from a modified Evo XL engine, and only a sports bike could get away with the huge and efficient air cleaner and muffler.

The VR-1000 has only a trace of H-D heritage: It's a 60-degree V-twin and water-cooled. At the end of six years of competing in the AMA Superbike series, the VR's best finish has been second, twice.

Model year 2000 brought the FDXD, the sports Dyna, with dual front brakes, cast wheels, several shades of black, and an artful disguise of the balance tube joining the exhaust just behind the gearbox.

Continued from page 90

They were putting us on, because for the 2000 model year the Softails got the Twin Cam Beta engine, as the factory called it, a twin cam 88 except that the cases had been enlarged to fit a pair of counter-rotating balancers. The original rubber-mounts and then the Twin Cam Alpha, so to speak, didn't cure the vibrations. They isolated the riders from them. But the Beta engine cured the shakes, a truly amazing and impressive feat of engineering.

The cloud that accompanies this 1990s silver lining popped up in 1994, in the form of a road-racing program featuring a different sort of Harley-Davidson—the VR-1000. It's as different a machine as anything

New for the model year 2000 was the Deuce—(a play on numbers and words both), a Softail with the counter-balanced beta version of the Twin Cam 88 engine and a new, conservative sense of style.

seen at Juneau Avenue (the company's corporate headquarters in Milwaukee) since that WJ Sport of 1919.

The VR-1000 is a 1,000-cc, racing-only Superbike, although H-D fudged the rules by declaring the model a production bike, getting it certified by the Polish government! It uses overhead cams, water cooling, and is a V-twin with a 60-degree included angle.

None of the other racing teams have objected to its questionable certification, because the VR-1000, after five years, is still hopelessly slow. It's never won a race; it's

never even come close despite the team hiring top riders for the kind of money you'd expect to pay a top guy who's about to spend a season being blown into the weeds.

The Motor Company has backed this project because the owners and managers believe in the future. When the next wave breaks, when Harley-Davidson needs to match Honda, Triumph, and BMW, motorcycle against motorcycle, when nostalgia isn't as good as it used to be, Harley-Davidson will have the plant and the people and the products they're surely gonna need.

Index